# Improving Education Together

# Improving Education Together

*A Guide to Labor-Management-Community Collaboration*

**Geoff Marietta**
**Chad d'Entremont**
**Emily Murphy Kaur**

HARVARD EDUCATION PRESS
CAMBRIDGE, MASSACHUSETTS

Paperback ISBN 978-1-68253-062-7
Library Edition ISBN 978-1-68253-063-4

Library of Congress Cataloging-in-Publication Data

Names: Marietta, Geoff, author. | D'Entremont, Chad, author. | Kaur, Emily Murphy, author.
Title: Improving education together : a guide to labor-management-community collaboration /
    Geoff Marietta, Chad d'Entremont, Emily Murphy Kaur.
Description: Cambridge, Massachusetts : Harvard Education Press, [2017] | Includes
    bibliographical references.
Identifiers: LCCN 2016058721| ISBN 9781682530627 (pbk.) | ISBN 9781682530634
    (library edition)
Subjects: LCSH: Educational change—United States. | Teacher participation in administration—
    United States. | Collective bargaining—Education—United States. | Labor-management
    committees—United States. | Community and school—United States. | School improvement
    programs—United States. | School management and organization—United States.
Classification: LCC LB2805 .M2825 2017 | DDC 371.2/07—dc23 LC record available at
    https://lccn.loc.gov/2016058721

Published by Harvard Education Press,
an imprint of the Harvard Education Publishing Group

Harvard Education Press
8 Story Street
Cambridge, MA 02138

Cover Design: Ciano Design

The typefaces used in this book are Scala and Scala Sans

# Contents

# Introduction

If you learned there was an intervention to improve student outcomes that worked for nearly all children across communities, what would stop you from using it? This intervention has closed learning gaps both in urban communities serving predominantly low-income minority students and in isolated rural areas with large numbers of white and Native American students living in poverty. It has worked in suburban, urban, and rural settings with white, African American, Hispanic, Native American, Asian, and multiracial students. That intervention is *collaboration*.

There is no doubt that collaboration is hard work in education. Stakeholders with diverse interests, backgrounds, and experiences must come together to develop solutions better than what they would have come up with working alone. While there is a growing body of research and resources on how to work together more effectively to improve student learning, educators often have a hard time finding relevant and accessible support. We have compiled this Guide on labor-management-community collaboration to bring disparate research and resources on collaboration together in one place for educators, community partners, and policy makers.

Most educational and community leaders know it is essential to collaborate, but do not know where to start. Online searches for resources on collaboration literally yield millions of results. The leader or practitioner motivated to collaborate is stymied by the sheer amount of information.

He or she has little time to sift through documents, watch videos, listen to podcasts, or attend webinars to learn how to get started or to deepen existing collaborative work. After seeing many powerful examples of how collaboration led to transformation in school districts, we decided to undertake this work. Motivated by the potential of collaboration as an effective and universal communitywide intervention, we took the time to collect, analyze, and curate as many resources on collaboration as we could find, including the best scientific research conducted at schools of education and business. The Guide is the collective result of our efforts.

The Guide illustrates tools and best practices using case studies of communities that have engaged in collaboration involving labor, management, and community stakeholders with the goal of accelerating student achievement. These case studies illustrate the challenges of collaboration as well as how stakeholders overcame those challenges using various protocols, processes, and resources. Although collaboration is rarely a linear process, the chapters build on one another. We begin by describing tools to assess readiness to collaborate and to form an effective team with diverse stakeholders. Subsequent chapters focus on the team process itself along with the problems of practice that are ideal for collaborative teams to address.

One of the first challenges of collaboration that we discuss is simply understanding what it means to collaborate. Collaboration so often means different things for different people. Some equate it with compromise, others with slow movement, while still others conceptualize it as the best way to build momentum and ideas that can be put into action. Collaboration also happens at different levels—among classroom teachers in the same school or between leaders across a community. To reap the benefits of what we call labor-management-community collaboration, it must be viewed as a *process through which stakeholders who see parts of a problem differently can explore these differences and construct solutions that are better than what they could have come up with on their own.*[1]

Our Guide focuses explicitly on labor-management-community (LMC) collaboration. This model emphasizes a collaborative decision-making process that includes community leaders and other partners in improving student outcomes. Parents, nonprofit leaders, government agency administrators, and business executives work with school system administrators, school board members, and union leaders on meaningful reforms that positively impact the learning relationship between teachers and students. In the LMC model, the community is an equal partner with labor and management in ensuring that students succeed in school and life. When labor, management, *and* community work together productively, there is tremendous opportunity to reduce redundancy, reallocate resources to more productive efforts, and create an expansive safety net for the most vulnerable students. Of course, broadening the number and diversity of school and district partners is not easy, but it has the effect of engaging a more inclusive team, producing results far greater than the sum of separate efforts.

## PUTTING COLLABORATION IN CONTEXT

Collaboration is hard to do and perhaps even harder to study. Until very recently, collaboration was often neglected as a topic of research. Some early work on the private sector looked at performance and innovation when businesses collaborated through joint ventures. These studies focused on the development and formation of joint ventures and their governance structures.[2] There is also considerable research on the preconditions necessary for high performance in private sector collaborations. Trust, common purpose, appropriate members, and adequate resources have all been identified as essential components.[3] In 2009, scholar and collaboration expert Morten T. Hansen wrote what many thought was the essential treatise on the topic in the private sector context. His book *Collaboration: How Leaders Avoid the Traps, Create Unity, and Reap Big Results* details successful examples of collaboration in the private sector and what managers could do to lead successful collaborative work.[4] While there is a solid body of research on private sector collaboration, the results from studies on collaboration in the public sector are just beginning to emerge.

For example, there is growing evidence demonstrating how effective collaboration between labor, management, and community stakeholders can lead to improved student learning. A group of early studies explored the factors that led to effective collaboration and hypothesized that productive labor-management relationships were a prerequisite to accelerated achievement.[5] Adam Urbanski, president of the Rochester Teachers Association and cofounder of the Teacher Union Reform Network (TURN), made a compelling case that any reform aimed at improving outcomes in teaching and learning must rely on teacher engagement and ownership. He wrote that without collaboration between administrators and the teacher unions, even the "best efforts of management are tantamount to one hand clapping."[6]

Subsequent research and reports attempted to quantify the effect of collaboration on student learning. Yet scholars' attempts to pinpoint the impact of labor-management relationships on learning have been thwarted by the complexity and diversity of policies and practices across states and districts.[7] In addition, there was a paucity of research on the topic, and results were mixed and inconclusive.[8] The only takeaway from these early studies was that labor-management collaboration seemed to matter, but no one was really sure how.

Notably, one report from the NEA Foundation published in 2007 attempted to show how districts could use labor-management collaboration to improve equity and reduce the achievement gap.[9] The authors tried to draw the link between enhanced collaboration and improved outcomes in Clark County School District in Nevada and Hamilton County, Tennessee. The report drew heavily from the concepts on "win-win" bargaining outlined in Kaboolian and Sutherland's 2005 work on building collaborative district-union relationships.[10]

Soon after the financial crisis hit in 2007–2008, stresses over how to spend depleted resources led to old fights between labor and management in an effort to control costs. The debate was often framed in zero-sum terms. Teachers could either absorb the cuts through reduced pay or job losses, or management could reduce central office staff and redirect funds to teachers. But at the same time, a third way emerged that began to recognize the importance of shared responsibility for shaping policy and making hard choices.

New research began to unpack the mechanisms of labor-management relationships and their effects on teacher capacity and student learning. In 2011, the US Department of Education compiled evidence of a positive impact on student achievement from twelve school districts in its *Local Labor-Management Relationships as a Vehicle to Advance Reform*. They found that districts with strong labor-management partnerships—Baltimore City Schools, Denver Public Schools, Hillsborough County Public Schools, and Montgomery County Public Schools, for example—were able to improve student achievement by collaborating on teacher evaluation, compensation, and career development systems.[11] Montgomery County saw double-digit closure in the gap between black and Hispanic students and their white counterparts in nearly every grade level in reading and math achievement. While multiple initiatives contributed to these improvements, many attributed that performance jump to productive labor-management collaboration.[12]

Similarly, McCarthy and Rubenstein analyzed the labor-management relationships in a cross section of urban and rural, large and small districts to better understand how to enhance planning, decision making, and problem solving in districts and schools. Their two studies, published in 2011 and 2014, included thirty schools in California serving 1,100 students (46% free and reduced lunch) and found that higher-quality partnerships between management and labor, as well as more frequent and extensive communication, led to improved student performance. The authors show how labor-management collaboration in these districts was created and sustained to improve overall teacher quality and accelerate student achievement.[13]

Drawing from examples in Cincinnati, Ohio, and Union City, New Jersey, Anrig (2013) explained how teachers and administrators codesigned curricula, professional development, and evaluation systems to improve student performance. The results in Union City have been remarkable. In a district with nearly 11,000 students—96 percent Hispanic and 85 percent low-income—language arts and math proficiency nearly matched or outperformed statewide averages in 2013. Compared to Hispanic and low-income students in New Jersey, Union City children had double-digit leads in academic proficiency.[14]

The reports were complemented by how-to guides and frameworks for district and union leaders.[15] *Working Better Together* was published as a comprehensive manual for leaders in the public sector to build more effective relationships with employee groups.[16] The US Department of Education developed its own conceptual framework and principles for building productive district-union collaboration.[17] Some states, such as Massachusetts, put forth their own efforts in advocating for enhanced labor-management relationships.[18]

Despite their demonstrated success, the number of meaningful partnerships in the country is modest, and most only involve labor and management. And this is not because collaboration is unnecessary. Quite the contrary, collaboration is critical for solving complex social problems—poverty, gun violence, abuse, and educational inequality. Some research studies suggest that humans may even be predisposed to collaboration.[19] These and other social struggles cut across organizational, political, geographical, and ideological boundaries.[20] Indeed, in our experience working with communities in Massachusetts and elsewhere, we have found that enduring solutions can only be devised when labor, management, and community stakeholders work together.

Kania and Kramer lay out the characteristics of deep communitywide collaboration, which they call "collective impact."[21] This type of collaboration is defined by long-term commitments by a group of important actors from different sectors—teacher unions, school districts, businesses, and community organizations—to a common agenda for solving a specific social problem. We were motivated to write this book with the goal of increasing and expanding deep collective-impact LMC collaborations. We will not make significant progress addressing educational inequality in our communities until all stakeholders are working together productively.

Of course, the criticisms and questions about the tradeoffs of LMC collaboration must also be acknowledged. For example, Moe (2006, 2011) has written extensively about the disproportionate amount of influence teacher unions have on politics and educational policy in the United States.[22] In addition, Brill (2012) has raised awareness about dysfunctional teacher dismissal policies that he attributes to the self-interests of teacher unions.[23] More importantly, there are practitioners on the ground who are skeptical that the benefits of collaboration outweigh its costs. Some superintendents and principals may think collaboration erodes their authority and capacity to lead. Teacher union leaders might believe collaboration means capitulation or "selling out." Ordinary teachers may feel overwhelmed, undervalued, and frustrated, and may be unsure the investment in collaboration will change anything. It is important to keep these concerns and practitioners in mind when moving toward LMC collaboration. However, in this Guide we emphasize collaboration as a decision-making process involving labor, management, and community stakeholders as equal partners.

## How to Use This Book

Given the stubborn achievement gaps still in evidence across the country, the potential of and need for collaboration is tremendous. The challenge for leaders and practitioners is how to best stimulate effective collaborative action. Different organizational goals, cultures, procedures, and languages create barriers to success.[24] Furthermore, intentionally integrating community stakeholders in reform efforts increases the complexity. Although district managers and union labor leaders have different roles, they do work in the same system. Daily or weekly contact often occurs in carrying out everyday duties, making collaboration much easier. Community members—parents, nonprofit representatives, business leaders, and others—must not only put in extra efforts to learn what is going on, but must also take time off work and away from their family to do so.

Unfortunately, practical and accessible resources on how to overcome these barriers and collaborate effectively are hard to find. Teachers, administrators, and community partners are often unaware of the rising tide of research and reports on labor-management collaboration. And even those who know of the research often struggle to make sense of it at a more practical level.

This Guide walks educational and community leaders and practitioners through a step-by-step process of getting collaboration started in their communities, or of expanding and deepening existing efforts. The early chapters are designed primarily for communities just beginning on the road of LMC collaboration; those well on their way with collaborative efforts can use the first part of the book to refine and strengthen their work. Resources and examples in these chapters focus on understanding the end goal (chapter 1), identifying the starting point with a needs assessment (chapter 2), and ascertaining best practices for forming a diverse multi-stakeholder team (chapter 3). Later chapters address developing effective team processes (chapter 4), selecting a meaningful problem centered on improving student learning (chapter 5), and knowing what to do when things go wrong, particularly after an agreed-upon solution begins to be implemented (chapter 6). The districts and communities featured show a particular tool, process, or concept in action. Our goal is to make LMC collaboration as real and tangible as possible by showing examples of how it works in real-life situations.

In chapter 1 we start first with a basic understanding of collaboration and what it means to partner on meaningful reform with a broad group of community stakeholders. This sets the foundation for applying processes and tools to reach the end goal of effective collaboration, *when stakeholders construct solutions that are better than what they could have come up with on their own.* Chapter 1 describes Baltimore's route to a new teacher evaluation system to illustrate collaboration between schools, unions, and community members. Baltimore's collaboration illustrates the features of a robust, collective-impact collaboration because it engages a broad coalition of stakeholders to address critical aspects of student learning, such as teacher compensation and professional development.

Once you have an understanding of effective LMC collaboration, it is critical to then assess readiness to collaborate. Chapter 2 illustrates tools and resources to do just that, using case studies on communities in Springfield, Massachusetts, and La Grange, Illinois. A comprehensive and transparent needs assessment lays the foundation for collaboration by identifying stakeholders' differing views on major issues. Those involved in the collaboration can then begin reconciling how their perspectives align or diverge. This process is critical to arriving at specific strategies that people doing the work feel engaged with and are willing to implement.

Once stakeholders understand their differing perspectives and readiness to collaborate, it is time to form the team (if one doesn't already exist). Chapter 3 provides best practices on forming and facilitating LMC collaborative teams by highlighting work in Fall River, Massachusetts. In this chapter we emphasize that team recruitment must be thoughtful, intentional, and attentive to the identified problems. Given that most teams will be responsible for bringing an improvement project from design to implementation, it is important, during team formation, that considerable attention be given to including those individuals who will be responsible for sustaining the work, including community members, principals, and teachers. Although taking time to understand the working styles and skill sets of each team member can seem like a distraction, evidence suggests that teams that slow down, cultivate good norms, and build a sense of trust and understanding prior to commencing the work lay a more solid foundation for collaboration.

Chapter 4 focuses on strengthening and sustaining an effective process for collaboration once the team has been formed. There is a saying that "process trumps strategy." The reason for this is that the environment is always changing, and strategies must respond to those changes. Process is critical to responding and recrafting an effective strategy in a timely manner. We advocate for taking a problem-solving approach that uses the features of interests-based bargaining. In chapter 4 we provide tools and resources on how to use an interests-based process (IBP) to maximize outcomes by prioritizing relationships and promoting structures meant to build and expand trust.[25] Facilitators (either internal or external) are key structural elements and are there to encourage participation in problem solving among all team members. IBP emphasizes transparent information sharing, jointly chaired committees, and the identification of shared interests.

The hallmark of any successful collaboration is that the stakeholders are working on a problem that is specific, meaningful, and connected to student learning. Chapter 5 illustrates how the needs assessment (chapter 2), team (chapter 3), and process (chapter 4) come together to identify a specific problem that is critical to improving student outcomes. Using a case study of the school system and community in Revere, Massachusetts, we show how a well-defined and important topic not only motivates people to engage in collaborative work, but also helps team members get through difficult times. Working on meaningful reforms also brings in a wider and more diverse group of stakeholders. The challenge is identifying an issue that is important, connected to learning, and within the locus of control of stakeholders.

Collaboration rarely goes as planned. In chapter 6 we address what to do when collaboration goes wrong (which it will) in implementing agreed-upon solutions. Leaders come and go, elections produce unexpected results, and external shocks, such as budget cuts, introduce new tensions. Such disruptions can undermine and even lead to the suspension of collaborative activities. It is critical in any collaborative process that participants expect challenges and do not give up when they occur. To get through difficult times, stakeholders must understand that implementation occurs in stages and is a continuous process. It requires teams to establish clear ground rules for communication, procedures for individuals to join and leave collaborative projects, and formalized structures, such as joint labor-management committees, that extend shared decision-making processes beyond personal relationships.

Throughout the book, in end-of-chapter appendixes, we provide a number of practical tools and resources to engage in collaborative decision making. However, our Guide is not exhaustive. There may be some resources not covered that stakeholders find helpful. Moreover, we do not expect users of the Guide to find every resource valuable. The Guide might be viewed more as a menu than a recipe. There are plenty of options to choose from to help enhance or initiate collaboration. The big challenge is moving from collaborating on specific issues or topics to developing a system of continuous improvement grounded in a collaborative culture.

## NO CHOICE BUT TO COLLABORATE

It is no longer a choice whether to collaborate. In an increasingly globalized and service-based economy, collaboration is growing and will continue to do so. Organizations in our knowledge-based economy tend to thrive, or fail, on their ability to work in teams, learn, and innovate. Those who succeed cultivate a diversity of perspectives, engaging committed professionals in a process of continuous improvement to achieve shared goals.[26] In education, the effectiveness of any recent reform, such as Common Core, teacher evaluation, and new school-choice models, is inextricably tied to the ability of school board members, superintendents, principals, teachers, the union, and community leaders to work together. Our goal is that this Guide will make the experience of working with others more effective, and help collaboration reach its full potential as a cross-setting policy intervention.

# CHAPTER 1

# *Understanding Collaboration*

T HE FIRST STEP TO ENGAGING in labor-management-community (LMC) collaboration is having a clear and shared understanding of what collaboration means and what it looks like. We've seen over and over again how slight misunderstandings in the beginning of the LMC process lead to bigger problems down the road. Some equate collaboration with compromise, others with negotiation. Only with a common definition of collaboration can labor, management, and community leaders move through this step-by-step Guide and use the tools and frameworks effectively.

In one community, for example, school board members and administrators often used the term "collaboration" when discussing their contract negotiation with the local teacher union. From the teacher union's perspective, the often contentious negotiation was usually anything but collaboration. When the groups sat down together with community members to plan a joint initiative, the first few meetings got off to a rocky start. As administrators talked about collaboration on the project, teacher leaders were reminded of the traditional bargaining process and assumed they would be asked to give up something in return for anything they wanted in the initiative. The community members involved could sense the discord, but not put their fingers on it. It was not until one member of the group asked everyone what they meant by "collaboration" that the differing perspectives came to light. To the administrators, collaboration meant coming to agreement on the contract; for the teachers, collaboration was a zero-sum game of compromise. Once people's various notions of collaboration were articulated, and they had come to a common definition, the group could move on and refer back to that definition during critical decision points.

Of course, this example just highlights that collaboration often has as many different definitions as people involved in the actual collaborating. In the example, administrators were using the term to describe collective bargaining. Collective bargaining—the legal contract negotiations between an employee group (teacher union) and management—could potentially involve collaboration, but often it does not (at least according to our definition of this term). Similarly, collaboration between management and labor can take many forms, but certainly does not require formal contract negotiations. Collaboration between management and labor can range from open communications and transparency on day-to-day topics, to the creation of single or multiple labor-management teams or projects, to the inclusion of teacher leaders in key decision-making processes of a school or district, to the formation of policies and structures that embed collaboration in the fabric and daily practice of the district. For this reason, the very first step in the process is to create a common understanding of collaboration and how the process will be structured to include and empower different groups.

As stated in the introduction, we define collaboration as *a process through which stakeholders who see parts of a problem differently can explore these differences and construct solutions that are better than what they could have come up with on their own.*[1] Collaboration is not just compromising by agreeing to some middle points between two positions, but expanding possibilities by adding other parties with different perspectives who can help find new and creative solutions. Such an approach offers rich possibilities to guide educational policy, particularly in the complex realm of collective bargaining. In the case of LMC collaboration, we view stakeholders involved in collaboration as the legs on a three-legged stool. Each leg—labor, management, and community—represents a different perspective generally based on the role they play in solving problems to improve student outcomes.

Labor includes the teachers, assistants, service workers, and specialists who are tasked with the day-to-day care and instruction of students. Labor stakeholders spend the most time in direct contact with students, and therefore are often well attuned to their strengths and needs. They often have the best understanding of what will and will not work to improve outcomes. In many cases, labor stakeholders will elect someone to represent their interests through an organized teacher or service employee union. The union president, vice president, or other executive then typically serves as the representative leader of labor stakeholders, particularly in collaborative efforts that concern the district or community as a whole.

Management is typically composed of principals, administrators, superintendents, and school board members. They are tasked with implementing federal, state, and local policies designed to meet societal, political, and economic goals. In collaborations, the superintendent or her designee is often the stakeholder representative for management.

Community stakeholders encompass a large and very diverse group that may represent parents, businesses, nonprofits, and other government agencies. Of the three groups, community stakeholders are often the least represented in LMC collaboration. Two factors make the inclusion of community stakeholders difficult. First, the community stakeholders represent wider and more varied interests than those typically found in labor and management. For example, imagine how the perspectives might differ (or overlap) between a local business owner concerned about finding qualified candidates to fill entry-level positions, a pastor at a nearby church wanting to grow a congregation, and a parent on the parent-teacher association who has a teenage son with autism spectrum disorder. The diverse perspectives of community stakeholders make eliciting feedback and engaging in a long-term collaborative process challenging. How can (or should) all community perspectives be brought to the collaboration table in a meaningful way?

A second challenge with regard to involving community stakeholders has to do with their proximity to the school district's day-to-day work. Labor and management representatives often work within the same school system. They know many of the same people, and focus daily on improving student outcomes. Community stakeholders may be employed in an entirely different industry, and not be familiar with best practices in education. Complicating matters is the phenomenon that everyone was at one point a student in a classroom taught by a teacher. Consequently, most community stakeholders have a perspective—informed or otherwise—as to what constitutes quality instruction.

For these reasons, some believe that involving community members in meaningful collaborative efforts makes work more difficult, and is not worth the payoff. We argue the contrary. By involving the community early on, labor and management leaders can avoid costly design mistakes that need to be reversed or drastically altered in future years, such as school redesign, new construction, or teacher compensation. Partnering with the community also builds goodwill to support bond referendums or tax increases that bring additional resources to the school system, and leverages untapped experience and resources that can improve student outcomes. As a third leg in the stakeholder stool of LMC collaboration, the community can support greater and more comprehensive reform efforts that accelerate increases in student outcomes.

But in order to work together productively, the people representing each of these diverse perspectives must have a common understanding of what it means to collaborate. In this chapter, we first present a basic working definition of collaboration that includes its five key features. We then show how these five features vary in different types of collaborations. Finally, we illustrate the features of collaboration in a case study of work in Baltimore City Schools. With labor and management leaders working deeply together, Baltimore City Schools developed a remarkable and innovative new teachers' contract that eliminated the traditional "steps-and-lanes" pay scale. Simultaneous efforts to engage parents and community members led to a successful bond issue that delivered $1.1 billion for school construction and repairs. By engaging in LMC collaboration across the community, Baltimore City Schools was able to lay the foundation necessary to significantly improve student learning. The real challenge and potential will be when all three stakeholders—labor, management, and community—join together to address a common problem or challenge. In this way, the case shows the potential of LMC collaboration, but also the challenges of fully engaging the community with labor and management stakeholders.

## FIVE FEATURES OF PRODUCTIVE COLLABORATION

Creating shared understanding requires a very clear description, and we use the definition of collaboration provided by expert Barbara Gray, a professor of organizational behavior at Penn State and the director of the Center for Research in Conflict and Negotiation. As a trained and experienced mediator, Gray has worked with hundreds of collaborations around the world involving seemingly intractable situations, particularly around environmental issues. Gray is a recognized expert on collaboration, and her 1989 book *Collaborating: Finding Common Ground for Multiparty Problems* is one of the formative texts on the topic. According to Gray, collaborations have five key features, as described below.

- *Interdependence.* Stakeholders are interdependent. They rely on each other to get work done and accomplish goals. One member of the collaboration could not solve the problem without the support and help of the others.
- *Joint solutions.* Solutions to problems emerge as the stakeholders work through their different conceptions of the problem. This feature is best illustrated with the blind men and elephant parable. A group of blind men touch an elephant to learn what it is like. One who feels the trunk says the elephant is like a tree branch. Another touching the side of the elephant explains that it is like a flat wall. A

third touching the tusk remarks that the elephant is like a smooth
pipe. Only when the blind men can come together and communicate clearly does an accurate description of the elephant emerge.

- *Ownership in decisions.* There is joint ownership of the decisions
  made by the stakeholders collaborating. Stakeholders are engaged
  in the decision-making process. They feel included in the decision
  and are willing to defend it to critics.
- *Responsibility for outcomes.* Stakeholders assume collective responsibility for the outcomes of those decisions. When things go wrong
  or right, stakeholders are willing to accept responsibility. Blame or
  praise is felt and accepted equally across stakeholders. There is no
  lone scapegoat.
- *Dynamism.* The collaboration process is emergent and dynamic.
  The size, composition, and focus of issues develop over time.
  Communication and problem-solving strategies become more
  refined and responsive. There is a sense of continual progress.

To summarize, collaboration involves interdependent stakeholders developing solutions to problems, over time, so that they all feel responsible
and accountable for the outcomes. For example, LMC collaboration could
be a group of teacher union leaders, district administrators, parents, and
local business owners who work together to develop joint monthly professional development sessions. This is what happened in Montgomery
County, Maryland, where the teacher union president and vice president
worked with school district leaders and local business executives to form
the Montgomery County Business Roundtable for Education (MCBRE).[2]

The stakeholders involved in MCBRE jointly planned and implemented
monthly professional learning sessions targeted for school, union, and business leaders. In one such effort, the joint group examined ways the district
could improve the productivity of some of its business processes. Dubbed
"Operation Excellence" or "OpEx," the group created joint district-business

task forces, doing its best to match the skill sets of the companies and individuals involved, to look at four specific district management areas: strategic planning, facilities, finances, and technology. After meeting for five months, the group published a report of sixty-three recommendations to improve systems and processes. For example, for facilities the LMC collaboration recommended that the school system develop standard operating procedures for all school plant equipment maintenance functions, develop a complete inventory of equipment at each site, and reassign the Indoor Air Quality team to the Division of Maintenance.

In practice, collaboration occurs along a continuum of the five features—interdependence, joint solutions, ownership in decisions, accountability for outcomes, and dynamism—that is tied to impact.[3] As mentioned in the introduction, Kania and Kramer describe the most impactful type of collaboration as collective impact, which is the ultimate goal for LMC collaboration. This involves a long-term commitment between diverse stakeholders who share ownership in decisions and use a common measurement system to track progress.

The example of Baltimore, Maryland, illustrates the power of LMC collaboration to achieve collective impact. Specifically, in the following section, we use Baltimore City Public School's 2012 contract negotiations with the local teacher union, as well as its efforts to engage parents in the process, as models to better understand the features of collaboration, how they connect to collective bargaining, and the roles of labor, management, and communities. The Baltimore City Schools case is unusual in that collaboration was used to create an innovative new evaluation system that created options for career pathways for teachers that based pay on performance and peer review.

Moreover, collaboration became an integral part of collective bargaining in Baltimore. In and of itself, this is an impressive feat. What makes this case even more unusual is that collaboration became part of the implementation process, as outlined in the contract. In this way, the collaboration resulted in a long-term commitment to the process by a diverse group of stakeholders.

## COLLABORATION IN BALTIMORE, MARYLAND

In the fall of 2012, then-superintendent Andres Alonso sat in his office reflecting on his tenure over the last five years as CEO of Baltimore City Public Schools.[4] Alonso had been successful in leading improvement in the district. High school dropout rates had declined by 55 percent; graduation rates had increased more than 10 percentage points; student performance had improved in nearly all subjects and grades; and the district had settled a twenty-eight-year-old federal lawsuit over special education services.[5] Most impressively, by employing features of collaboration, Alonso oversaw the approval and implementation of an innovative teachers' contract with a jointly governed four-tier career pathway that tied teacher pay and promotion to performance and peer review. The agreement was hailed as a "bold step to transform the city's schools" by American Federation of Teachers President Randi Weingarten. US Secretary of Education Arne Duncan commended Baltimore for "leading the nation in innovative contracts and making teachers real partners in reform."[6]

Despite these successes, Alonso had a troubled mind. His pioneering work to create career pathways for teachers faced significant obstacles, and Alonso was concerned about the future of the contract and the reforms it introduced. First, implementation had not gone smoothly, and there were worries that teachers were not transitioning to the new contract, which rewarded "engagement" as opposed to "passivity." Second, there were open questions about the rigor of the new pathways, and whether the best teachers were being selected for the "Model" pathway. Looming in the background was the union president's reelection and the expiration of the contract in the coming summer. A new leader could signal significant changes for the relationship between the district and the union.

In order to understand the lessons that the new career pathway in Baltimore City Public Schools (BCPS) offers for collaboration, we first examine how Alonso was able to work with the Baltimore Teachers Union (BTU) to negotiate and ratify a contract that revolutionized the way that staff were

evaluated and paid. We will follow with an examination of the early implementation, while the final portion of the chapter will focus on understanding collaboration as a way to find a pathway ahead.

## Contract Negotiations

Before Alonso negotiated the new contract, BCPS had used a traditional
"steps-and-lanes" salary schedule to determine teacher pay. Simply put,
teachers were paid based on their numbers of years of experience along
with their training. Teacher evaluation played no part in moving teachers
up the salary scale, and very few teachers were rated "unsatisfactory." In
addition, only about half of Baltimore teachers were officially evaluated in
2008–2009, and the district had initiated the dismissal process for only
about twenty tenured teachers (of approximately 4,400 total). Salaries for
new teachers in Baltimore were competitive, but as teachers proceeded
through their career, their salaries quickly fell behind those of other districts.
For example, teachers with a master's degree and twenty years of experience
in Baltimore could earn $10,000 to $15,000 more if they moved to Prince
George's or Howard Counties.

In order to address the salary discrepancy and evaluation problems,
Alonso proposed that BCPS replace its traditional salary schedule with a
career ladder including four pathways. At that time, Marietta English was
the president of BTU and governed with a twenty-one-member board. It
was English's job to protect the rights of the 10,800 BCPS employees serving over 84,000 students in nearly two hundred schools. When pre-nego-
tiation meetings began between Alonso and English in the late fall, English
was skeptical. Because the system being discussed was very different from
salary scales in other districts, it raised many questions for English, including ones about equity. These challenges were surmountable because of the
positive social capital that Alonso had already built with BTU. Alonso had
implemented significant reforms that pushed resources from the central
office to the school site. Support and accountability were delivered through
sixteen network teams and a complementary group of sixteen executive

directors, responsible for coaching and evaluating principals. This approach worked well with BTU (an affiliate of the American Federation of Teachers), the body that represented teachers, related service providers, and support staff in the district.

When negotiations began in January 2010, the two sides used a problem-solving approach with a "win-win" orientation, which focused on core interests and mutual benefit. The salary scale served as the starting point for the conversation. BCPS and BTU agreed to start with changing the salary scale, but they had different reasons for doing so: BTU wanted to shorten the number of steps on the pay schedule so that teachers could reach the maximum salary more quickly; BCPS wanted to eliminate paying for master's degrees.

Once Alonso had sketched out the framework for the contract and some of his nonnegotiables, he stepped back from the day-to-day proceedings. He only reentered the discussions when they reached an impasse. After a few negotiating sessions, the participants expressed serious doubts about whether the proposed plan was financially sustainable. To address concerns and skepticism, BTU engaged the help of financial experts from the American Federation of Teachers (AFT). In what the BTU considered an unprecedented move, Alonso opened the BCPS budget to an AFT financial expert. By sharing financial spreadsheets, both sides were working with the same assumptions about revenue and expenditures.

Assurances built into the contract helped both sides feel comfortable with the final agreement. For example, Alonso agreed to certify that the changes would be implemented or else the contract would revert to the old pay schedule. In addition, BCPS and BTU created joint governance structures through which both sides could continue talking—the policy-level Joint Oversight Committee and the implementation-oriented Joint Governing Panel.

The completed contract went to BTU membership for ratification in October 2010. However, members rejected it. They did not have enough time to make sense of its sweeping changes and there was a lack of adequate communication by the union. In response, the BTU turned to the national AFT for support, bringing in a "blitz" team to help them communicate to members. After a month-long campaign, a second vote was held in November 2010 and the contract passed with 65 percent of the vote.

### Implementing the New Contract

With the contract ratified, the new career pathways were on their way to implementation. Teachers could now progress through "intervals" within four "career pathways"—Standard, Professional, Model, and Lead—by earning "achievement units" and being reviewed by a "professional peer review committee." Although the contract provided the broad-stroke outlines of the new system, it left the details, processes, and rubrics to two joint district-union committees: the Joint Oversight Committee (JOC) and the Joint Governing Panel (JGP). It was their job to make the transition between the long-standing standardized steps-and-lanes pay scale to one based on career pathways, achievement units, and peer review. The JGP included eight teachers—four appointed by the district and four by the union—who were to work full-time to generate the many guides, protocols, and rubrics needed to implement the contract. During the first year, this included defining what it meant to be a "Model" teacher and then designing a rubric and assessment process to select such teachers. They also needed to design rubrics to specify what types of activities could be exchanged for achievement units.

Unfortunately, no one had bothered to update the timeline for implementation after the first vote on the contract had failed. Alonso, English, and their respective leadership teams had lost over a month trying to ratify the contract. By January, the JOC had developed an application process for the positions on the JGP and appointed eight district and union members to the committee. Challenges emerged for the JGP from its very first meeting. Three of the four BCPS members came directly from the classroom and had entered teaching through alternative routes—two through Teach For America and one through the Baltimore City Teacher Residency program. Not all had positive views of the BTU prior to joining the JGP. On the BTU side, three of the four members served on the BTU executive board.

Collaboration between the district and union-appointed members had an uncertain start. The difficulty of the work was intensified by the varying levels of understanding about the underlying principles of the contract. After several weeks of conflict, the entire JGP attended an off-site retreat to work out differences.

The JGP finally settled on a definition of a Model teacher. Members then had to begin what one member described as the "painful learning curve" of developing a rubric to measure those characteristics. A key question for the JOC and JGP was how BCPS could assess the performance of teachers with limited resources, particularly in the domain of instruction? The discussion quickly turned to whether teachers' instruction would have to be observed in some way to achieve Model status. Some members of the JGP thought that videotaping teachers' instruction was the best solution, but there was strong opposition from BTU representatives. After some heated discussions, the JOC eventually decided that teachers would have to submit a video of their teaching for the Model pathway.

Implementation of the new contract was ongoing. Through the summer and fall of 2011, BCPS implemented a pilot process for the first cohort of teachers to apply for the Model pathway. By the deadline in November 2011, 341 teachers had submitted complete applications. Of this group, one hundred scored 80 percent or better on the rubric and were promoted to the Model pathway.

More than two years after ratification, some pieces of the contract had not yet been implemented. Alonso, English, and their leadership teams had underestimated how much time it would take. Unfortunately, delays and challenges in implementing the contract were beginning to jeopardize its sustainability. A small but vocal group of related service providers—psychologists, social workers, audiologists, physical therapists—thought the Model pathway and processes were not appropriate for their positions. The district and union also still had to define the Lead pathway, and develop a rubric and process by which teachers could attain it. There were also concerns about the role of the principals in the new contract.

At this point Alonso was blazing a new trail, asking faith and patience of the BTU as they embarked on an experiment to replace the traditional steps-and-lanes structure with career pathways. There was no rule book on how to best work with BTU as this new experiment unfolded. Yet, because of the collaboration between the district and union, Alonso was able to keep the conversation open and make adjustments rather than give up when challenges were encountered.

### What About the Community in LMC Collaboration?

As leaders in Baltimore worked to obtain and enact the new contract, they made efforts to reach out to local community members and include them in the work and vision. Although these efforts were not specific to the contract negotiations, they were deep and impactful. Community collaboration efforts began when Alonso arrived in 2007. As one of his first major moves as superintendent he conducted a listening tour over months, using this as an opportunity to align himself with parents.[7] Deborah Demery, president of the PTA Council of Baltimore City and mother of a son in City Schools, agreed that Alonso welcomed conversations with families: "He had an open-door policy. If you had something that you felt wasn't right, or if you knew that there was a situation going on in the school where parents didn't feel that the climate was good for them, you would let him know, and things were put in place to help engage parents."[8]

After the listening tour, Alonso took action. He formed a comprehensive strategy for parent and community engagement. As a direct outcome, he hired an executive director for the district's new Office of Partnerships, Communications, and Community Engagement, combining three previously independent functions. The office established three core values to guide their work:

- Fair, clear, open decision making
- School freedom equals school responsibility
- Families as partners

Their strategy focused, in part, on initiatives that built the capacity of families and school staff to partner with one another, or more widely, to spur partnerships between community-based organizations (CBOs) and individual schools. The goal of the movement was to fully engage families and community members in the creation of "community schools" across the district.

The first step of the process was to target funding. Executive Director of Family Engagement Michael Sarbanes and his team began to build a network of CBOs to partner with schools using $500,000 of funds generated through a reallocation of the Office of Engagement's budget along with private foundation money. Thus began a new family and community engagement policy that shifted real decision-making power to families and communities. The policy ensured that schools and CBOs were measured on a range of concrete actions involving the interaction of parents and schools.

As the policy went into place, guidelines were provided to build stronger relationships between schools and the community. For example, the revised policy required all schools to hold annual meetings for families and community members. The agenda for these meetings was prescribed by the regulations accompanying the new policy. Specifically, schools were required to hold annual open meetings where they would review school performance data, discuss school improvement plans, present budget priorities, and explain the school's implementation of its family and community engagement strategy. Schools were also directed to establish a "recognized, organized parent group if one does not currently exist," as well as a School Family Council to involve families and community members in school governance.[9]

Using their funds, Sarbanes also created a new position called the Family and Community Engagement (FCE) specialist. FCE specialists were assigned a roster of schools, where they were responsible for providing technical assistance and acting as a liaison between the schools, communities, and central office. Schools that went through a planning process earned the designation of "community school." Each community school also had one community-based partner organization and a full-time coordinator, paid for by a combination of city, school, and state funds, coordinated through the community organization Family League.

By May 2014 there were forty-three community schools in the district and an additional twenty-two undergoing the planning process.[10] Broader indicators also suggested that the combined efforts had led to greater community engagement. As the community became increasingly engaged, there was also greater advocacy and organizing efforts to lobby the state for money to rebuild and renovate schools. Multiyear efforts led by community-based organizations and parents resulted in rallies—often involving thousands of parents and community members—advocating on behalf of schools.

Ultimately, the voices of CBOs and families led Baltimore City, with the support of the mayor and elected state representatives, to pass a bill to deliver $1.1 billion for school construction and repairs. At the end of the 2013 legislative session, the bond bill passed both houses with large bipartisan majorities. In May 2013, then-Governor Martin O'Malley signed the bill into law, guaranteeing funding to build fifteen new schools and renovate twenty more. This victory highlights the reciprocal benefits of schools partnering with the community.

## THE FEATURES OF COLLABORATION

By inviting a diverse group of stakeholders to work together on important problems facing the school system, including the state of the school buildings, Alonso was able to unlock the potential of collaboration for collective impact. The case of Baltimore illustrates how the five features of collaboration—interdependence, joint solutions, ownership in decisions, accountability for outcomes, and dynamism—can be leveraged over the long term to improve student outcomes. However, getting all three stakeholders on the same reform effort moving in the same direction is a very difficult goal, particularly without clear resources to point the way. In the following sections we examine their efforts to better understand the pieces of the process that were successful, and how deepening the connection to community stakeholders as part of an LMC collaboration could have resulted in even better outcomes for the students of Baltimore.

### Interdependence and Joint Solutions

There is tremendous opportunity when labor, management, and community work together productively. Typically, when community members and organizations partner with a school or a district, they do so through their ties to a single entrepreneurial leader in the system—frequently a principal, a teacher, or a central office administrator. Broadening out the number and diversity of school and district partners is often not easy, but it has the effect of engaging a more inclusive team, typically including labor and management. By creating interdependence between labor and management in the new career pathway system, leaders in Baltimore were able to generate joint solutions that were better and more resilient than those devised by one group working alone. At the same time, community stakeholders were noticeably missing in that effort.

Indeed, bringing in community actors can be particularly helpful at certain stages of an improvement process. The additional resources and expertise might have been particularly useful as BCPS and BTU looked to undertake the work of creating the systems and structures of the new pathways. There may well have been corporations in place in Baltimore that had addressed tricky issues of performance evaluation that could lend expertise and experience to the process. Funders might be willing to add resources to the process. By explicitly planning to widen the circle of stakeholders, BCPS and BTU could further strengthen their work.

### Ownership and Accountability

In far too many cases, the stakeholders engaging in collaboration do not assume ownership for their decisions, nor do they feel accountable for the consequences of those decisions. In the case of Baltimore, district and union leaders felt ownership for their decisions because they made them together. Furthermore, they were responsible for defending those decisions to their respective constituencies. This simple act of advocating and defending decisions leads to accountability for results. When the model pathway process worked (or didn't), members of the JGP and JOC felt accountable for the success (or failure).

### Dynamism

As Alonso progressed from the idea of a new system of performance evaluation and pay to contract negotiations to implementation, the needs of collaboration changed. The dynamic and emergent nature of collaboration was evident. What the BCPS case illuminates clearly is that negotiating and ratifying the contract is only part of the collaboration process. By creating conditions that required ongoing collaboration—such as the creation of the JOC—Alonso established the necessity for stakeholders to work together to devise joint solutions. The members of the JOC and JGP were interdependent; they relied on each other to get work done and accomplish goals. Just as importantly, collaboration is a process through which parties who see different aspects of a problem can constructively explore their differences and search for solutions that go beyond their own limited vision of what is possible.

This case illustrates not only how collaboration can transform collective bargaining between labor and management, but also how leaving out community stakeholders can weaken even the best-laid plans. The goal is to move beyond bargaining as the major touchstone in labor-management relations, and toward a deeper and more sustainable communitywide collaboration that includes all stakeholders.

The purpose of this chapter has been to understand what it means to truly collaborate, and particularly to achieve a collaboration with a long-term collective impact, bringing together all the diverse stakeholders needed to achieve a successful reform. A fully formed understanding of collaboration is essential to effectively using our Guide. The tools, processes, and approaches in the following chapters all have the end goal of producing deep collaboration between diverse labor, management, and community stakeholders. Understanding what that collaboration means and looks like is the critical first step of the journey.

# CHAPTER 2

# *Are You Ready?*

## CONDUCTING A NEEDS ASSESSMENT

THE END GOAL OF LMC COLLABORATION is a situation where you and the stakeholders engage in reform efforts and develop solutions that you all feel responsible for making, with outcomes for which you all share accountability. With this purpose in mind, the next step is to understand your starting point. To use the tools, processes, and protocols of this Guide effectively, it is essential to know two things up front: where you are starting, and where you are going. In this chapter, we explain how a needs assessment will help you understand your starting point, and why it is a critical first step toward LMC collaboration. We then describe several needs assessment tools created specifically for education, and show them in use through two case examples.

Successful collaboration requires a shared vision for meeting agreed upon goals—a vision that may incorporate personal interests and agendas, but is not beholden to them. In education, this often means identifying specific strategies for improving student learning outcomes, such as peer assistance and review or extended learning time. But before engaging in collaboration around these and other improvement strategies, it is essential to assess readiness to begin. A comprehensive and transparent needs assessment lays the foundation for LMC collaboration by identifying the differing views of stakeholders concerning the major issues. Those involved in the collaboration can then begin reconciling how their perspectives align or diverge. This reconciliation process is critical to arriving at specific strategies that people doing the work feel engaged with and are willing to implement.

Needs assessments can take on many different forms and may be aimed at multiple audiences. A needs assessment might involve surveys, focus groups, and interviews with teachers, parents, students, community members, administrators, and board members. Although the process and audience might be very different across communities, a successfully implemented needs assessment serves to identify the following critical building blocks of LMC collaboration.

- *Baseline facts and performance data.* A needs assessment should highlight baseline facts and performance data to ensure there is a common understanding of how students and teachers are performing within the context of particular targets or goals. Performance data help ground difficult conversations in specifics, and allow stakeholders to talk about challenges without blaming one group or another. Conversation can then focus on the students' needs (e.g., fourth-grade students' literacy proficiency) rather than personalities or leadership in the school or system.
- *Readiness to collaborate.* Readiness is all about the relational starting point between stakeholders. Needs assessments evaluate readiness by answering key questions such as "What is the level of trust between key leaders?" Understanding the general perceptions stakeholders have of each other, particularly their degree of trust, helps educators make smart choices about how and when to collaborate. When readiness is imbalanced or one group lacks trust in another, stakeholders must be thoughtful and intentional about initial steps.
- *Perceptions of problems.* An effective assessment also identifies perceptions of problems (and strengths) in the system. In some cases,

stakeholders may see that they agree on particular problems. But there is almost guaranteed to be at least some disagreement about which problems create the biggest barriers to improving student outcomes. For example, teachers might cite a lack of support or resources as one of the biggest problems they face, whereas parents might perceive a lack of communication and awareness as a fundamental challenge in their child's education. An effective needs assessment will help stakeholders see what problems they perceive and how those perceptions differ. Armed with that information—and an understanding of basic performance and readiness—educational leaders can start the hard work of LMC collaboration.

Of course, implementing a needs assessment is not a one-day or one-week process. Simply asking teachers, parents, administrators, or community members how much they trust a particular stakeholder group or what problems they face is not a productive approach. Assessing readiness and perceptions of problems means asking the right questions in ways that elicit open and honest answers. People must first trust that the needs assessment process will take their input seriously and treat it with respect. This means that assessing the key building blocks of collaboration takes time and resources. Fortunately, there are a number of tools that can help educators and leaders make the right decisions when conducting a needs assessment.

In this chapter, we will introduce and examine tools designed to aid needs assessments. These include Consortium for Educational Change's System Assessment and the National Education Association's KEYS 2.0 survey. Throughout the chapter, we draw on examples of communities that have conducted successful needs assessments, and point out some of the lessons they learned in the process. We will then present an example of how teachers, administrators, district leaders, and community members created new visions for learning using needs assessments in Springfield, Massachusetts, and La Grange, Illinois.

## THREE REASONS WHY THE NEEDS ASSESSMENT
## PROCESS MATTERS

A thoughtful and well-planned assessment not only provides data that stake-holders need to start at the right place, it also helps deepen collaborative efforts down the road. The needs assessment does this in three ways. First, it builds buy-in early on in the process. Second, the needs assessment helps create or communicate a sense of urgency across stakeholders. Third, the process, if done correctly, establishes transparency in current and future collaborative work.

### Builds Buy-in

Before describing the specific tools, it is important to understand why a needs assessment is critical to building buy-in for greater collaboration. There is an adage that helps explain the role of the needs-assessment process: It is hard to burn down a house that you helped build. Indeed, this was a favorite saying of Jerry Weast, the former superintendent of Montgomery County Public Schools in Maryland, who helped unite three labor unions, parents, community organizations, and businesses in an effort to improve student outcomes in the district. From his perspective, the needs assess-ment was one of the first steps—the foundation—of building that house of collaboration in the Montgomery County community. The assessment helped establish dialogue about important features of the "house"—size, design, location, features, rooms, style, and so on. As problems were identi-fied through the assessment, stakeholders had critical conversations about what it meant when a group did not agree on fundamental aspects of learn-ing, such as having an expectation that all students can learn.

In the process of building buy-in through a needs assessment, it is essen-tial that participating stakeholders go beyond simply talking about different features they would like in the house they are building. Stakeholders with differing points of view must feel like their ideas were incorporated into the overall design. People must feel like their voice was not only heard, but also acted upon. Nothing can inhibit or destroy trust more in the house-building process than eliciting input and then not acting.

## Creates a Sense of Urgency

Before LMC collaboration can happen, people need to think that it *has* to happen in order for things to improve. Collaboration is very hard work. Without a real sense of urgency for change, educators, parents, community leaders, and administrators will stay in their silos and do the work they know. The needs assessment can play a crucial role in creating an urgency for change, particularly if there is one group of stakeholders who may think things are just fine. The process of identifying readiness and perceptions of problems often elicits conversations that begin with "Wow, I didn't know that was such a serious problem" or "I feel like we need to do something now or we'll lose our community." Those statements start building the case for why LMC collaboration is needed, and why now. Indeed, management guru John Kotter has studied the change process for decades.[1] What he learned is that for any type of major change to happen in an organization, the first step is to create urgency. Without urgency, there is no change or collaboration. The needs assessment can help create that urgency in a productive way that opens a learning process for all stakeholders.

## Establishes Transparency

Transparency in terms of how the needs assessment will be done is critical to obtaining the honest input needed for successful collaborations. In situations where there is little trust between stakeholders, or where that trust is just emerging, a misstep can set things back months or even years. The needs assessment is an opportunity to establish confidence in the collaboration process from the beginning. Thoughtfully designed assessments allow for anonymous reporting and do not force stakeholders to provide potentially identifying information. Name and contact information should always be voluntary. In addition, in a small school or department, grade level, job title, and years of experience can often be tracked back to specific people. The real problem with not guaranteeing anonymity is not so much that leaders would track down specific respondents and harass them for saying one thing or another (although that may be a legitimate concern in some circumstances). Rather, the big problem is that if people do not feel that their responses are anonymous, then they will not be honest on the needs assessment. Without everyone's honest answers, it will be impossible to identify readiness or problem perception, and the entire collaborative process could be jeopardized.

One way to safeguard anonymity and establish transparency is to have a diverse group of stakeholders develop and implement the needs assessment. As described in the next section, this is what leaders did in Springfield, Massachusetts, when they used the National Education Association's KEYS 2.0 survey for their needs assessment. When Springfield began the assessment process, they formed a KEYS 2.0 implementation team composed of representatives from all stakeholders in and outside of the school system. These included not only typical players such as union leaders, board members, administrators, and parents, but also community members.

One word of caution is needed before conducting a needs assessment. Many communities may not be ready to conduct a systemwide assessment. In the case where the risk is too great or there is not enough capacity, stakeholders may consider engaging in bridging activities that help build buy-in, establish urgency, and generate trust. A smaller-scale needs assessment at the school level or focused on a particular neighborhood might be the best place to start. Alternatively, the community or district may target a needs assessment around one particular need. For example, if the school system recently went through a strategic planning process, stakeholders may choose one or two of the identified growth areas to focus on for a needs assessment. Such an approach demonstrates that the system is taking the strategic planning process seriously by acting on findings. It also allows other diverse stakeholders to provide their input in the process.

## NEEDS ASSESSMENT TOOLS

There are a number of different tools you can use to assess collaboration readiness and perceptions of problems. We focus on two research-based and well-tested tools in this chapter: National Education Association's KEYS 2.0 survey and Consortium for Educational Change's System Assessment. Both have been used for needs assessments by dozens of different districts in communities across the United States. However, the KEYS 2.0 survey and System Assessment are not the only two options available for communities. Some larger systems have taken on the challenge of developing their own assessment. Although time-consuming, developing an assessment in-house has the added advantage of customizing questions specifically to community needs. In addition, the development process itself can help build buy-in, create a sense of urgency, and establish transparency. In the chapter appendix, we provide a summary of the various needs assessment tools. Before jumping directly to the tools, though, we recommend reviewing the KEYS 2.0 or System Assessment processes as illustrated in the following cases, which include best practices for process and content for needs assessments. In addition, you will likely find that both are broad enough in scope to address any particular issues you might have in your district, school, or community. We begin here with a description of the KEYS 2.0 survey.

## KEYS 2.0

The National Education Association (NEA) has put together its own research-based assessment called KEYS 2.0, which has been used successfully by a number of districts to jump-start collaboration. Initially designed with teachers in mind, the survey has been successfully used with other stakeholder groups such as parents and community members. The survey is comprised of forty-two indicators that measure perceptions of six keys to school improvement work (see figure 2.1). In the survey, stakeholders answer 250 questions covering five to eleven indicators for each of the following six keys:

1. Shared understanding and commitment to high goals
2. Open communication and collaborative problem solving
3. Continuous assessment for teaching and learning
4. Personal and professional learning
5. Resources to support teaching and learning
6. Curriculum and instruction

**FIGURE 2.1**    Six keys and 42 indicators

### KEY I. Shared Understanding and Commitment to High Goals

1. Shared goals for achievable education outcomes are clear and explicit.
2. Teachers, administrators, education support personnel, and other school employees take responsibility for the achievement of challenging standards for all students.
3. Curriculum is student centered.
4. School operates under the assumption that all students can learn.
5. School district administrators support staff efforts and monitor progress toward achievement goals.

### KEY II. Open Communication and Collaborative Problem Solving

1. In a climate of non-threatening, two-way communication, school administrators and staff collaborate in problem solving.
2. Parents are involved in and support the work of the school.
3. Teachers, administrators, education support personnel, and other school employees collaborate to remove barriers to student learning.
4. Teachers work closely with parents to help students learn and improve education.
5. Teachers discuss standards and approaches for curriculum and instruction.
6. Teachers are involved in decisions about student learning.
7. Teachers are involved in decisions about school operations.
8. Parents, community, and staff other than teachers are involved in decisions about school goals.
9. Teachers communicate regularly with each other about effective teaching and learning strategies.

### KEY III. Continuous Assessment for Teaching and Learning

1. Student assessment is used for decision making to improve learning.
2. Academic programs are assessed regularly.

**FIGURE 2.1** Six keys and 42 indicators *(Cont.)*

---

3. Assessment results have consequences for students and staff.
4. A variety of assessment techniques are used.
5. School programs are consistent and coherent.

## KEY IV. Personal and Professional Learning

1. Professional development has a direct, positive effect on teaching.
2. School administrators and staff work together to provide relevant professional development experiences.
3. Teachers are prepared to use state or district curriculum assessment or performance standards.
4. Classroom observations and constructive feedback from teachers and principal are included in professional development.
5. Teachers are prepared to address the needs of students with diverse learning needs and backgrounds.
6. Teachers have regularly scheduled time to learn from one another.
7. Staff development opportunities are pursued through organized professional development activities within and outside the school.
8. Staff development is provided in the areas of decision making and problem solving.
9. Staff development is consistent, comprehensive, and related to practices in the school.
10. Opportunities are available for mentoring.
11. Teachers have strong knowledge of their subject matter areas.

## KEY V. Resources to Support Teaching and Learning

1. Computer hardware and software supplies are adequate for students and teachers.
2. Support services are adequate.
3. Space for instructional activities is adequate.
4. The school provides a safe environment for learning.
5. Academic resources are adequate.

## KEY VI. Curriculum and Instruction

1. Curriculum includes "learning how to learn" activities.
2. Varied, engaging, collaborative strategies are used in instruction.
3. Curriculum provides opportunities to study topics in depth.
4. Curriculum includes attention to accuracy and detail.
5. Instruction includes interventions for students who are not succeeding.
6. Students are provided with personal instruction and feedback.
7. Research conducted at school influences programs and instruction.

---

*Source:* Andrew Churchill and Sharon Rallis, *Using KEYS 2.0 District-wide: A Springfield, Massachusetts Case Study* (Amherst, MA: University of Massachusetts Center for Education Policy, 2009).

Results from the KEYS 2.0 survey then show the district or school's average and standard deviation on each indicator and key (see figure 2.2) as compared with answers on the survey from other schools in the community. It also includes the average and 90th percentile in a national validation study. Several case studies document the survey's use to improve labor-management relationships, including one on Springfield Public Schools in Massachusetts.[2]

### KEYS 2.0 in Springfield, Massachusetts

Context is critical to understanding the role that the KEYS 2.0 needs assessment played in facilitating LMC collaboration in Springfield, Massachusetts. The city was declared insolvent in 2004 following a long decline in its

**FIGURE 2.2**    Key I Shared understanding report example

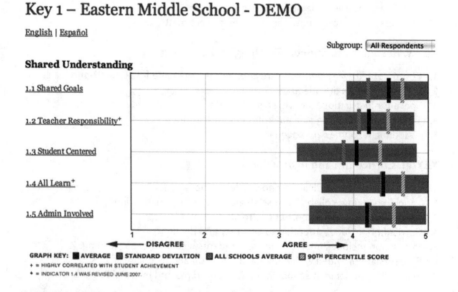

*Source:* Andrew Churchill and Sharon Rallis, *Using KEYS 2.0 District-wide: A Springfield, Massachusetts Case Study* (Amherst, MA: University of Massachusetts Center for Education Policy, 2009).

manufacturing-based economy, reduction in state aid relative to other cities, failed attempts at new job creation, and years of mismanagement and corruption.[3] The state provided an interest-free loan of $52 million, and Springfield avoided bankruptcy. But, as a condition of the loan, a state-appointed board took over all aspects of the city government, including its public schools.[4] When the board took over in July 2004, teachers had been without a contract and had not received a pay increase for two years.[5] At the same time, a significant increase in the percentage of low-income students attending Springfield Public Schools was putting strain on the system's resources.[6] To top it off, student achievement was amongst the lowest in Massachusetts.[7]

Over the next few years, the problems facing Springfield appeared to worsen. Teachers fled the uncertainty, stress, and low pay for nearby districts; after the first year of board control, the district experienced its largest exodus of licensed teachers in a single year. Specifically, in the 2005–2006 school year, Springfield Public Schools was forced to hire nearly six hundred new teachers, representing 15 percent of the total teaching force. A majority of these new teachers hired were not licensed or considered highly qualified under standards set by No Child Left Behind.[8] Thus, when Springfield implemented the KEYS 2.0 survey to assess its readiness to collaborate and understand perceptions of problems in the district, there was a polarized relationship between administrators, teachers, parents, and community members (see figure 2.3).

In response to the crisis and contention, the superintendent and union president agreed to form a joint committee to address some of the complex and serious problems facing the district. The joint committee was a seven-member team composed of three union members, three district representatives, and a school board member, designed to create action plans to improve district-union collaboration.[9]

To the members on the team, the next natural step was to assess the current situation in Springfield. Team members of the joint committee wanted to know first if everyone was ready to work together, and if so,

**FIGURE 2.3**   Challenges facing Springfield Public Schools when collaboration emerged

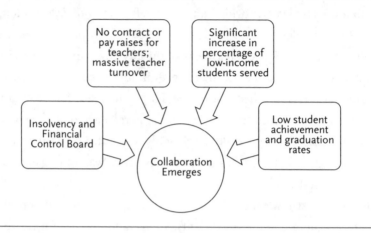

what problems should be prioritized. They discussed different options for a needs assessment and decided that a survey was the best route to gathering detailed information on all the schools in the district, efficiently and transparently. They reviewed several different surveys before selecting the NEA-designed KEYS 2.0. Given the strained relationship between teachers, administrators, and community members, the leaders of the committee knew that transparency in the process was critical to eliciting honest responses. Therefore, the team announced the KEYS survey in a joint letter to all staff members from the superintendent and teacher union president. The letter explained that the survey was anonymous and supported by both the administration and union leadership. Even so, some teachers were unsure their answers would actually be anonymous. The union took the additional step of traveling out to schools to help administer the online survey and answer any questions that came up. It should also be emphasized that agreeing to use a needs assessment tool developed by the nation's largest teacher union was seen as an important gesture by both labor and management. Such initial acts of faith can set a positive and trusting tone for future discussions and decisions.

In the end, over 80 percent of district teachers and administrators completed the forty-five-minute survey. To analyze the data, the team expanded to include twenty members with district, union, and community representation. The first few meetings were divisive; teachers and administrators spent most of the time blaming each other for the school-based problems highlighted in the survey.[10] After twenty-five hours of meetings and many difficult conversations, members of the expanded committee finally reached consensus. They decided to focus on three areas they believed were critical to student success that showed a need for improvement in the Springfield schools: 1) schools should operate under the assumption that all students can learn; 2) they should provide a safe environment for learning; and 3) teachers should be involved in decisions about school operations.[11]

## Inconsistent Expectations for Student Learning

One of the more controversial findings that emerged from the data was that Springfield teachers had varying beliefs in their expectations for what students could learn. Initially, there were heated conversations on the committee about what exactly it meant that teachers and administrators had scored low on the indicator statement "school operates under the assumption that all students can learn." However, as the committee members unpacked their concerns and met with teachers in schools, they found the problem to be less about belief and more about preparation.[12] As noted above, there was a large increase in the percentage of low-income students attending its public schools, which in turn, put strain on the system's resources. In addition, student achievement was amongst the lowest in the Commonwealth. In 2004, only about half of students graduated from high school in four years, the percentage of students proficient or above in English language arts remained in the mid-30s for all tested grades (36, 35, and 32 percent in grades 4, 7, and 10, respectively), and only a quarter of fourth graders and fewer than one in ten eighth graders were proficient or above in math.[13] Teachers felt they did not have the skills and knowledge needed to meet the diverse learning needs of their students.

As members were having difficult conversations about teacher capacity, the district was beginning to implement a new comprehensive teacher evaluation system. An outgrowth of the contentious bargaining process, the new system created a new process for evaluating teachers and included the new roles of instructional leadership specialists and teacher leaders to help struggling teachers.[14] With the new evaluation system in place, the committee recommended that the district and union form a small working group to develop the rubrics, observation forms, and evaluation reports needed for the evaluation. This joint working team then created the evaluation instruments used for all district teachers, teacher leaders, librarians, and counselors. The district also asked the union to help train teachers and administrators on the new instrument. This joint implementation of the new evaluation reduced miscommunication and increased buy-in. As one union leader noted, "It ensured that principals and teachers were receiving the same message at the same time from the same people."

## Concerns About Unsafe Learning Environments

Another important concern raised by many teachers in the KEYS survey was the belief that some schools were not safe learning environments. Many new teachers struggled with managing classroom behavior. In Springfield, with its large percentage of new teachers, creating a safe learning environment became a districtwide issue. To address the problem, the union and district met to discuss various approaches to reducing problem behaviors across schools. Together they decided that the Positive Behavioral Interventions and Supports (PBIS) model met the needs of Springfield Public Schools' students and teachers.[15] To implement PBIS, each school formed a PBIS leadership team composed of the principal, teachers, and other staff members who made joint decisions about the school's culture.

## Lack of Opportunities for Shared Decision Making

The third concern identified by the KEYS data and highlighted for action by the committee was that Springfield teachers felt they had little say in how the district and schools operated. "The basic idea is for teachers to stop being the objects of reform," said the union president, "and start being the architects of reform." Incorporating teachers' voices into school and district decisions means including teachers or their representatives on senior leadership teams, a move some superintendents are hesitant to make. But the Springfield superintendent at the time had a different perspective. With a commitment to collaborating, he knew he would have to spend even more time with union leaders. The solution seemed simple: invite the union leaders to join him and senior district leaders on the districtwide Instructional Leadership Team (ILT). That would mean one less meeting and more time spent with union leaders to develop a better relationship. The superintendent explained his rationale by saying, "Time is the enemy. If you are trying to build a relationship with someone, then you have to spend time with them. You can't work in isolation to get the kind of results needed."

## The Community's Role

To the Springfield superintendent, the only way to ensure that improvements lasted beyond any one person's tenure was to make the community an equal partner in the process. As the superintendent at the time said, "Real education reforms are developed by the community with buy-in." With the expansion of the KEYS 2.0 and ILT efforts, the leaders in Springfield generated an LMC collaboration plan, called the Springfield Collaboration for Change, that integrated parent-teacher home visits, summer learning initiatives, and joint district-union school leadership teams, while also increasing collaborative structures at the district level. The goals of the plan were twofold: deepen collaboration at the school level and increase parent and community engagement. To begin, Springfield Collaboration for Change focused on building collaborative school leadership teams, providing school-based support coaches, and scaling up parent-teacher home visits to reach more families. The plan's implementation was led by a leadership team with representatives from the school system, teacher union, community foundations, health and employment government agencies, and other community organizations.

Within a year of implementation, the impact of the LMC collaborative initiative was starting to emerge. Principals were beginning to see that teachers who went on home visits were changing the way they taught, and parents were becoming more engaged in the school. One principal explained, "It's basically a relationship-building experience . . . Parents are more apt to share with us information about their children. They are more relaxed to ask questions about school. It builds an overall collaboration that really is essential for student achievement." This was particularly important in Springfield, where students did not necessarily attend schools located in their own neighborhoods. "A lot of our students are bused in and don't live nearby," explained one teacher, "so it's good for a teacher to go out and see where they live . . . and for parents to see that their teachers really want to help them and their child." Similarly, parents felt better informed about what was going on in school and how they could help support learning. One father stated, "Before, I never knew what was going on; I never knew anything. I would just pick her up and leave. Now I come in and say 'Hi.' You see people, you know people."

Impact was also reaching beyond the classroom. At the district and community level, the Springfield Collaboration for Change brought a new level of resource coordination to Springfield. With leaders from the five major organizations funding or leading work with children, the leadership team could quickly see overlaps between programs, gaps in services and opportunities to partner. Perhaps most importantly, the initiative helped build widespread support for quality education and services for the children in Springfield. As the superintendent remarked, "Community collaboration helps build public trust and confidence. It is in the community's best interest to work with schools."

## Consortium for Educational Change System Assessment

Another powerful needs assessment tool was developed by the Consortium for Educational Change (CEC). Established in 1987, CEC is a network of Illinois school districts with a consistent mission to build collaborative structures, processes, and cultures to transform educational systems to continuously improve student learning and achievement.[16] CEC has been helping communities and school systems go through a needs assessment process, called System Assessments, since 1998. The System Assessment is a comprehensive method of organizational self-study, written assessment, site visit by a team of peer educators who conduct interviews and analyze the system's data, and collaboratively written feedback based on a continuous improvement framework. It integrates organizational and professional learning frameworks, such as the Baldrige Performance Excellence Criteria, the Characteristics of a Professional Learning Community, and the Five Essentials for School Success.

From 2008 to 2015 CEC helped carry out over a hundred System Assessments across the state of Illinois. There are five specific purposes for the assessment, but the basic goal is to evaluate readiness for collaborative reform and identify problems preventing improvement in student outcomes. The System Assessment offers a planned way of identifying gaps in organizational performance based on performance excellence criteria. Communities, schools, and districts then have an external validation of the data gathered, from which they can learn strengths and areas of opportunity for use in planning for future improvement.

### The System Assessment Process

The first step in the process of conducting a System Assessment is to assess whether a group of stakeholders is even ready to do one (see figure 2.4). Implementing and benefiting from a System Assessment requires a base-level commitment to collaboration. The typical starting point is with the district administration—the superintendent and senior leadership—although some System Assessments have been jump-started by school board members or engaged community leaders. According to veteran educator and senior CEC leader Perry Soldwedel, it is absolutely critical that districts and communities be committed to working together on the process for the System Assessment to be effective. As Soldwedel says, "We don't do anything unless there is a strong labor-management relationship. All must sign on because the relationship is built on always looking at what is working and how to get better." Indeed, Soldwedel points out that of the hundred-plus System Assessments that have been completed, only two have been "shelved" by participants. In both cases the problem was due to readiness. In one district the superintendent, senior leadership, and union president were all ready. But the board and some community members were not. They viewed the district as already high performing—96 percent of students were meeting state benchmarks—and didn't want to have the System Assessment identify weaknesses to the community. In another case, the superintendent who had been there a number of years was retiring. The board wanted to do assessment before the superintendent left and use the tool as a way to inform hiring. However, when the new superintendent came in, he ignored the findings from the report. (Two years later, however, he brought it back out and revised it.)

Sometimes everyone is committed to the process, but they need some time getting ready. The System Assessment uses best-practice research-based criteria of what a high performing school or district should look like. If the district is not familiar with it, then they need that foundation first. Stakeholders must first make connections with each other through criteria to create a common vocabulary. That process includes assessing readiness to collaborate. According to Soldwedel, stakeholders must answer the questions, "Do we value and appreciate each other? Do we realize that unless we work together we are not going anywhere?" In some cases, they find that there is a dark cloud hanging above the relationship. Soldwedel emphasizes that the cloud "needs to be lifted before engaging in the needs assessment."

**FIGURE 2.4** CEC System Assessment process

**SET UP: CEC**
- Identify district or school and verify its readiness.
- Identify district or school's Site Coordinator.
- Develop a project timeline.
- Finalize contract for the assessment visit.
- Identify Assessment Team members and CEC Team Leader.

**PRE–SITE VISIT: CEC TEAM LEADER**
- Provide district or school with introductory information.
- Identify three Focus Area Contacts and Self-Study Teams.
- Meet with Self-Study Teams to ensure understanding of the self-assessment process.
- Ensure Self-Study Teams complete self-study documents and post to the district or school website.

**SITE VISIT: CEC ASSESSMENT TEAM**
- Assessment Team meets to discuss self-study data and information.
- Assessment Team conducts interviews to verify/clarify self-study.
- Assessment Team identifies strengths, opportunities for improvement, and suggested next steps.
- Team Leader presents Oral Report of overall strengths and opportunities for improvement.

**POST–SITE VISIT: CEC TEAM LEADER**
- Team Leader synthesizes team input into written feedback reports.
- District or school receives the final written feedback reports.
- Team Leader returns to provide information and support for findings and to answer questions/defend the report.
- CEC, Assessment Team, and the district or school debrief the System Assessment process to make suggestions for continued improvements.

Once a community or district is committed to working together on the System Assessment, the next step is the actual diagnostic process. The diagnostic process includes a survey, self-study, and an external peer-led team visit. Each step is designed to collect data relating to three major areas—focus on learning, focus on collaboration, and focus on results—and then document the current situation. The district is encouraged to make the survey and self-study a stakeholder-driven process that includes community members, parents, and students. Once the district conducts the self-study and survey, it sends the data to the external peer-led System Assessment team prior to their visit. The team then reviews that data and prepares for their site visit.

During the actual site visit, a group of six to eight peer educators from outside the community visit for a period of three days to conduct interviews and collect data. All are volunteers except for the team leader. As a first step, the team holds an organizational meeting to meet key leaders, review roles and responsibilities, set the site schedules, and discuss their review of the data. They are then divided into three groups corresponding to the major areas mentioned above: focus on learning, focus on collaboration, and focus on results. Each subgroup is responsible for collecting evidence and determining strengths and areas for improvements for their assigned categories to share with the team (see figure 2.5).

On day two of the site visit, the team interviews stakeholders to see if their perceptions about what is going well in the district and what needs attention match the perceptions expressed in the self-assessment and the opinions/expectations expressed by leaders in the day-one interviews. Some examples of those interviewed include teachers, parents, students, support staff, and community members. On the third day of the site visit, the team meets to process all information. They then conclude with an oral exit report to senior leaders in the district and community. The report includes overall strengths and areas of opportunity. A written report follows in two or three weeks. The report includes strengths and areas of opportunity in each of the three main areas. The team leader then works with the district to develop an action plan that addresses recommendations. In the following

**FIGURE 2.5** Excerpt from Focus on Learning assessment

| Focus on Learning: We acknowledge that our fundamental collective purpose is to help all students achieve high levels of learning and therefore we are willing to examine all of our practices in light of their impact on learning. | 1 | 2 | 3 | 4 | 5 |
|---|---|---|---|---|---|
| | READINESS | PLANNING | BEGINNING | PROGRESSING | SUSTAINING |
| **A Guaranteed & Viable Curriculum** | | | | | |
| A. *Establishing the curriculum*: We articulate student learning outcomes across all classrooms to build shared knowledge regarding state standards, district curriculum guides, trends in student achievement, and outcomes for the next course or grade in all subject areas. | | | | | |
| B. *Executing the curriculum*: We ensure that each teacher gives priority to the identified learning outcomes in every unit of instruction to guarantee that each student has equal access to instruction that addresses those learning outcomes in all classrooms for the grade level or course. | | | | | |
| C. *Clarifying and communicating the curriculum*: We ensure that every teacher is able to assist all students and their families in knowing the essential learning outcomes so they can assist in monitoring performance in relationship to those outcomes. | | | | | |

*Source: CEC System Assessment Guidebook: Professional Learning Community Framework* (Lombard, IL: Consortium for Educational Change, 2015).

section, we give an example of what System Assessment process looks like in a school district.

### System Assessment in La Grange District 105

Located in suburban Chicago, La Grange District 105 serves approximately 1,500 students in five schools. There are four neighborhood elementary schools and one middle school for seventh and eighth graders. Almost half the students qualify for a free and/or reduced lunch, and one in five is an English language learner. Over the last ten years, enrollment in the district has exploded—an increase of 50 percent since 2005—putting pressure on facilities, human capital, and instruction. The largest growth has been in the Hispanic population. Ten years ago Hispanic students made up 25 percent of the overall district; that figure is now 40 percent. Given the rapid enrollment growth and changing demographics, Superintendent Dr. Glenn Schlichting could see there was a compelling need to adapt the district's strategy. Schlichting first engaged with CEC in 2009 when he reached out to Soldwedel about the System Assessment process. At that time, Schlichting was most concerned about the role of the board and administration, flat student achievement, and high teacher turnover. The issues were mostly internal, so Schlichting contacted CEC about doing a district-focused System Assessment. As the superintendent remarked, "We were looking for a road map, something that could focus on alignment in the district."

The district went through the System Assessment process as described above. Schlichting and his team prepared and put together the pre-visit data. Then an external team visited and interviewed teachers, principals, administrators, parents, students, and some community members. According to Schlichting, the process and final report led to better alignment and clearer goals in the district. As he said, "It was such a powerful experience; the process is not top-down and gives you a different perspective."

Three years later Schlichting felt that the district was ready for a communitywide strategic planning process. Once again, he turned to the System Assessment to drive the communitywide inclusive process. The district formed a thirty-five-member committee to provide input and become engaged in the assessment. Composed of teachers, parents, students, community representatives, and board members, the committee held retreats and regular meetings for six months prior to beginning the System Assessment. The outcome was a two-page plan to guide a System Assessment that examined needs at the school level. Another System Assessment was then conducted, which identified unique and common needs across the schools. The needs schools had in common were taken as district priorities.

To Schlichting, the positive consequences of the work are unmistakable. In a recent survey, 98 percent of staff say that they understand and support district-level goals and priorities. The school board has also responded with greater accountability and engagement. Every meeting they report on goals and progress. The board also updates action plans quarterly. As Schlichting says, "The strategic plan lives and breathes."

There were a few pieces of advice that both Schlichting and Soldwedel gave to other districts wanting to pursue a needs assessment such as the System Assessment. First, everyone involved has to have a mind-set of improvement and learning. People must be willing to not only receive celebrations, but also areas of need. There is also a lot of preliminary work that goes into a successful needs assessment. Stakeholders must build up a common language and understanding. As Soldwedel says, "The key question is, does it make a difference which school a parent would send his or her child to? Communities must ask themselves, 'Do we have a system of schools—with individual schools that perform very differently? Or do we have a school system?'"

## CHALLENGES TO KEEP IN MIND

There are a number of challenges to keep in mind when conducting a needs assessment. First, there is often a disconnect between practitioners and leaders in the school system as opposed to members of the community. The daily flow of information and decisions inherent in carrying out one's job gives those working in the school system a different experience with the needs assessment. They will naturally have more information and a deeper understanding of the process than community members. It is essential that administrators and teacher leaders move forward at the pace of community stakeholders. Community members will need more time to understand the implications of the needs assessment process and results.

A second challenge concerns the perceptions participants have of who is leading the process. Very often collaboration and the needs assessment process is driven by one or two key leaders. Although these catalysts may be critical to starting and sustaining the process, they must be very careful not to limit others' involvement and responsiveness. When others perceive that the so-called collaboration is dominated by one or two individuals, then the impact of working together will be quite limited.

Finally, and most importantly, it is critical to understand what it means to be "ready." Unfortunately, there is no cut-off score that says you are proficient in trust and ready to collaborate. Readiness is truly in the eye of the beholder. But if your efforts to get a needs assessment going do not succeed, or if the needs assessment identifies serious challenges (e.g., significant mistrust), then we recommend pursuing other activities that build buy-in, create a sense of urgency, and generate trust. These might include working together on a more focused needs assessment or choosing a tractable and agreed upon problem to address. If even these suggestions sound impossible, then we might suggest taking the advice leaders gave us in one district that was trying to build a more collaborative relationship in the context of deep distrust: invite your counterpart over to your house for a barbecue and say, "I really want to try to work together. How can we make this happen?"

The needs assessment is the beginning of the LMC collaboration process. Undoubtedly, it will yield more information than you can use. The next step is to work together through a team process to close in on what is most important. In order to do that effectively, it is essential to form a team using best practices. That is the topic of our next chapter.

# Appendix (Chapter 2)

## Needs Assessment Resources

*Tool 1: NEA KEYS 2.0* Developed by the National Education
Association, this is a comprehensive research-based survey tool
measuring forty-two indicators of school quality clustered around
six "keys." Results are presented in bar graphs that illustrate the
level of consensus among survey takers, how the school compares
with all schools that took the survey, as well as schools at the 90th
percentile on the scale.

*Tool 2: CEC System Assessment* The Consortium for Educational
Change, serving a network of Illinois public school districts, created this assessment tool aimed at helping a district or school identify strengths and opportunities for improvement aligned to the
effective practices of one of the continuous improvement frameworks. The System Assessment involves self-study, an external
peer review, an oral report, and a written final summary report. For
more information, see http://cecillinois.org/programs-services/
system-effectiveness/system-assessment/.

*Tool 3: Wilder Survey for Collaboration* To assess the readiness of
large multi-stakeholder groups, a group at the Amherst Wilder
Foundation has compiled a comprehensive research-based
questionnaire that identifies the key factors in effective collaborations. The questionnaire asks stakeholders to rate the readiness of their collaborative group on six dimensions: vision,

goals, communication, composition, purpose, and resources. Respondents score each of forty statements on a range from Strongly Disagree to Strongly Agree. The survey results provide a score for each dimension. For more information, see https://www.wilder.org/Wilder-Research/Research-Services/Pages/Wilder-Collaboration-Factors-Inventory.aspx.

*Tool 4: Organizational Health Index* This tool is used across industries to measure the strengths and weaknesses of management practices, and the overall health of labor-management relationships. For more information, see http://solutions.mckinsey.com/index/solutions/organizational-health-index.

*Tool 5: Statewide climate surveys* Some states also implement their own surveys to understand the climate of learning in schools and districts. Massachusetts, for example, conducts the statewide Teaching, Empowering, Leading, and Learning (TELL) survey to understand if teachers have the supports they need to help students learn. For more information, see http://www.tellmass.org/.

# CHAPTER 3

# *Building Capacity to Team Effectively*

ONCE THE NEEDS ASSESSMENT IS COMPLETED, the next step is to think about how to form a team to address the identified needs and move forward. And there is more at stake than just effective LMC collaboration. A growing body of evidence suggests that complex systems, such as school districts, grow and improve when their teams grow and improve.[1] One such study, by the Rennie Center for Education Research & Policy, found that creating a culture that prioritizes teaming, collaboration, and teacher leadership is integral to initiating and sustaining improvement.[2] Rubenstein and McCarthy found a significant positive relationship between schools that had labor-management partnerships and student achievement, indicating that students do better when people within schools are working together.[3] Leading organizational management scholar Amy Edmondson and the father of Improvement Science Tony Bryk have also documented the importance of teaming in creating a culture that learns quickly, adapts regularly, and innovates often.[4] In short, students benefit when teams work productively.

Of course, not everything has to be a team endeavor, and even a culture that supports strong teams needs individuals who are willing to take on leadership roles and get work done. A rule of thumb is that teams make sense when the problem and/or solution at hand is an interdependent activity that requires the expertise of, communication between, or commitment from multiple actors to effectively implement.[5] Since these are increasingly common factors in today's education environment, it makes sense to invest time and resources in creating a system with strong teams that can drive improvement.

With numerous studies as evidence that teaming and collaboration are a core part of improving teaching and learning, a critical question remains. How can districts, teacher unions, and community stakeholders form effective teams to both initiate and sustain improvement? In this chapter, we first review recent research on the characteristics of effective teams. We then identify five core strategies that form the foundation of productive team interactions. These strategies are illustrated through a case example of Fall River, Massachusetts, which embarked on a labor-management initiative with the goal of creating a districtwide learning culture through the use of professional learning communities. At some point or another, every effective team must be prepared to handle conflict. Indeed, productive conflict is at the heart of team effectiveness. Thus, we conclude the chapter with a discussion of techniques for managing conflict within teams.

## WHAT MAKES AN EFFECTIVE TEAM?

A large case study called the Aristotle Project was conducted by Google in 2012. This study gathered data on 180 teams of Google employees to assess why some had better outcomes compared to others. Interestingly, teams that ranked the highest did not necessarily have the smartest or the most powerful people on them, but instead had good team processes and a "good culture."[6] But what is "good culture," and how is it created on teams?

In the Aristotle Project, a positive team culture was associated with two qualities, which other studies have also cited.[7] First, effective teams have individuals who know when to speak up and how to listen effectively—meaning that team members share airtime and each member speaks for relatively the same amount of time. This act of conversational turn-taking ensures that no one person dominates the group, and that no members fall silent and fail to contribute. The second quality of positive team culture is a sensitivity or empathy toward other people's feelings.[8] Teams that demonstrated social sensitivity toward group members' feelings generated confidence amongst team members, which encouraged the sharing of new, innovative ideas that could then be vetted through the team process.

These two factors—conversational turn-taking and social sensitivity—do not represent groundbreaking findings. Indeed, they are tightly linked to a phenomenon that psychologists and organizational leadership scholars have been studying for years, called psychological safety. Psychological safety is the extent to which the team atmosphere builds intergroup trust.[9] A climate rich in psychological safety is one where team members feel free to voice opinions without fear of retribution or rejection, know and express interest in each other as people, believe each other to be competent, and assume positive intent.[10]

Research suggests that an environment rich in psychological safety, where team members trust each other and encourage risk-taking, is a principle predictor of team learning, improvement, and innovation.[11] So the big question is, how to create a team environment that is rich in psychological safety? In the following section, we will explore five key strategies that can help teams create a psychologically safe culture where members feel empowered to ask difficult questions, share data that shows there is a problem, suggest alternatives, and challenge the way things are done.[12]

## Creating the Foundation for a Good Team Culture

In our experience, there are five core strategies that help teams establish effective group dynamics to guide work so that it is collectively determined, designed, and implemented. These strategies are:

- Establish a compelling team purpose based on the needs assessment

- Compose the team thoughtfully and intentionally
- Create space and time to team
- Generate team norms
- Clearly define roles and responsibilities

It is important to note that the strategies are not necessarily outlined in a set order—where you need to complete strategy one before moving on to strategy two. You should think of these strategies as guidelines for teaming; while some strategies will happen in a linear pattern, others can be done concurrently. For example, the first strategy of establishing a compelling purpose for the team is directly linked to the both the needs assessment (chapter 1) and strategy two, team recruitment. This is the case because the issues identified in the needs assessment should drive the purpose of the team, which in turn should influence who is on the team. That is, the composition of the team may alter as its purpose is refined.

### Strategy One: Establish a Compelling Team Purpose Based on the Needs Assessment

The purpose of the team should be directly linked to the issues or problems identified in the needs assessment. Of course, establishing the purpose of the team likely requires a group of stakeholders working together to both define the problem and make an agreement to work together toward its resolution. That said, those involved in identifying the problem may not be the same team of people tasked with coming up with solutions. Moving from the needs assessment to establishing a team purpose is a delicate, iterative process of going from problem identification, to team purpose, to team selection. To address this challenge, some LMC collaborations will have a small core group of leaders define the problem, and then expand team membership to include more people who work directly on or have deep expertise in the identified problem.

No matter what process is used, the group as a whole should spend considerable time flushing out how that problem is perceived by all stakeholder groups. The team should build on the needs assessment and ensure that all stakeholder groups have input on identifying the problem and its root causes. In doing so, the team may consider using the so-called Five-Why process.[13] For each symptom of an identified problem, team members ask the question "Why?" until they reach agreed upon root causes. (Despite its name, there is no fixed number of questions involved in this process; the root cause may emerge after asking "Why?" two or three times, while in other cases it may take seven or eight times.) The Massachusetts Education Partnership has adapted this process to create an Understanding the Challenge protocol, featured in figure 3.1.[14]

Once a team is established, it is recommended that you share any data, community feedback, and the initial root cause analysis broadly with as many stakeholders as possible to create a unified understanding of the problem and to increase ownership. This also gives team members a chance to ask questions and clarify key points, potentially uncovering additional information that the smaller team may have missed.

### Strategy Two: Compose the Team Thoughtfully and Intentionally

Once a sufficient exploration of the problem has been completed, it is time to form the team (if one doesn't already exist). Team recruitment must be thoughtful, intentional, and attentive to the identified problem and its root causes. Given that most teams will be responsible for bringing their project from design to implementation, it is important during team formation or expansion that considerable attention be given to including those individuals who will be responsible for sustaining the work, including community members, principals, and teachers.[15]

The Education Delivery Institute (EDI), a leading organization in helping education leaders implement reform, outlines key factors to building a guiding coalition, which have been adapted to apply to LMC teams.[16] First, effective teams need to corral individuals with diverse perspectives and resources. This can include people from different levels of influence (e.g., district-, school-, classroom-level), stakeholder groups (e.g., teachers,

**FIGURE 3.1**    Example Understanding the challenge protocol

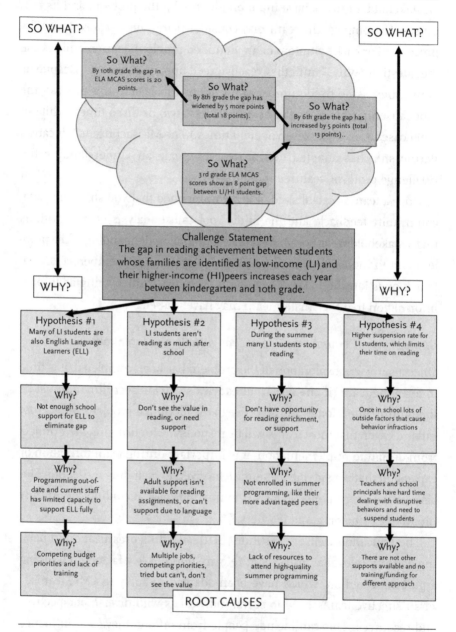

*Source: Understanding the Challenge* (Cambridge, MA: Rennie Center for Education Research & Policy, 2015).

community members, administration), and/or people who exhibit different types of authority (e.g., leadership, credibility, expertise).[17] This bringing together is important, as the more diverse your group is, the more alternatives will be generated and vigorously explored and, in turn, the better the potential solution will be.

Diverse people also bring with them diverse resources—time, space, money, and expertise—which can help accelerate progress.[18] Districts involved in the District Capacity Project, an initiative of the Massachusetts Education Partnership that works to build the capacity of labor and management leaders, were surveyed in June 2014 about their views on team diversity. They indicated that including the perspectives of labor, management, and community improved their ability to advance their efforts to establish and improve cultures of collaboration, and to make progress on their identified projects. Some team members and facilitators went further and suggested that they would encourage the team to include representatives from more diverse staff positions and school buildings.[19]

Secondly, although diverse groups in the long run have been shown to display more problem-solving prowess and creativity than their homogenous peers, it is not recommended that you bring random stakeholders into the mix. Instead, when responsible for creating a team, it is important to engage those people who you think of as having critical insight on the problem at hand, or on the potential solution. This typically means that labor, management, and community should be represented (traditionally in equal portions to avoid marginalizing one group). As one group of scholars from Harvard University's Public Education Leadership Project stated, "Providing structured opportunities for those in schools to shape and improve standardized practices will increase their effectiveness and enhance the commitment of those responsible for implementing them."[20]

Lastly, in addition to including diverse stakeholders, those responsible for creating the team should consider individual members' interest along with their ability to collaborate on the problem and solution at hand. This means taking into consideration both the individual's current commitments outside the group, their interest in the topic, and their interest in collaborating.[21] Individuals who have previously demonstrated that they possess a collaborative spirit, and who bring with them strong relationships with their colleagues, will help to bolster the effectiveness of the team internally as well as externally.[22]

### Strategy Three: Create Space and Time to Team

A commonsense but often overlooked requirement for productive teamwork is creating time and designating a space for the team to meet. Setting in advance a regular schedule for meetings takes the guesswork out of when or whether the team should convene. Meetings can always be canceled or rescheduled later if necessary. But trying to schedule a meeting month-to-month is a headache for everyone involved. We suggest setting a regular day and time each month for the team to meet. For example, the team might establish the first Thursday of every month to get together. And in our experience, steer clear of Mondays and Fridays for obvious reasons.

Just as important as finding a regular time to meet is also setting aside a comfortable space for the meeting. Ideally, the location would rotate between partners involved in the collaboration, and you may want to choose a neutral space for the first few meetings, particularly if there is little trust between the parties. We have seen examples where the space for an LMC collaboration team meeting became part of the undoing of productive work. In one large urban school district, a newly formed LMC team was given a windowless room that vented directly to a heavily used bathroom. At first, the space did not seem to matter as the members of the team were energized by the task at hand. But, as the year wore on, members began to notice the lack of natural light and constant noises of running water and flushing coming from the bathroom. Some members of the team began finding excuses to stay out of the working space, which inhibited the collaborative work.

Of course, even with a dedicated space and time to meet, eventually the success of the team comes down to whether members show up. Time is obviously the biggest constraint, and collaboration takes more time in the beginning. If people are resistant to scheduling what they see as yet another meeting that takes them away from the "real work," we suggest finding opportunities to use existing committees or teams for the LMC work. For example, if most of team is already part of a standing committee that meets regularly, why not just add the other members to that existing team, and then task the existing team with handling the problem? We have seen this work in several examples, and in most cases it means adding community stakeholders to joint labor-management committees.

### Strategy Four: Generate Team Norms

It is often difficult to do simple things, because not everyone has the same perspective on the things being done or the process for doing the work. When this happens, a platform for working as a team can be helpful. One simple framework for getting the work done is establishing team norms or ground rules for engagement. Creating norms in the following six areas can be particularly useful for teams looking to ground their work in a shared approach to teaming:[23]

- *Participants and attendance.* State your team's expectations around attendance, absences, team member exit or separation, how to handle meeting cancellations, or any other subject related to participation.
- *Meeting planning and record keeping.* Detail your approach to how you will plan meetings, create meeting agendas, and take and distribute meetings notes.
- *Interpersonal behavior.* List your team's agreed-upon norms of behavior that will create safe and open meeting environments; promote active listening, collaboration, and consensus building; build strong relationships; and avoid behaviors that might limit effective collaboration and teaming.
- *Communication with key stakeholders.* State your commitments about how you will communicate information about your work with

anyone outside your immediate team (e.g., district staff, members of your organizations, the community).

- *Decision making.* Define a decision-making process that will allow for joint problem solving, airing of concerns, consideration of all proposed options, and resolution by consensus.
- *Accountability.* Describe how your team will hold itself accountable to all ground rules listed above.

Norming is a great process for building a team culture, but it should not be done and then forgotten. In order to create a team culture that functions effectively and efficiently, it is often necessary to decide on a strategy for holding the team accountable to its norms. This can be done by posting or reviewing the norms at the start of each meeting, or having a "ticket to leave" at the end of each meeting that asks participants how well the team followed its norms. Springfield Public Schools in Massachusetts pursued the latter approach and created an end-of-meeting evaluation meant to quickly assess the culture of the meeting, how well the group followed its norms, and how productive the group felt it was (see figure 3.2). This strategy served not just to collect a bit of data that the group could then use to improve, but also to consistently remind the group of its norms and the direction toward which it aspired the conversation and group activity to progress.[24]

Please note, while established teams may choose to recycle norms, it is important to establish agreement from all team members that these recycled norms are still acceptable, allowing for changes or adjustments where needed.

The inquiry versus advocacy framework (figure 3.3) can be helpful to reference when creating your norms.[25] Inquiry is an open process designed to generate alternatives and ideas. It is a process where participants are actively asking questions and have not come to a conclusion on the subject. In contrast, advocacy is a process where participants are actively maneuvering to position their solution as the *best* option. Using an advocacy approach encourages discussion that is competitive and dominating.[26] Because an

**FIGURE 3.2**    Springfield end-of-meeting norm assessment

## Springfield Leadership Team
## Norms and End of Meeting Evaluation

### NORMS

- We will ask and raise tough questions
- We will check for understanding and agreement
- We will take risks, make mistakes, let go
- We will encourage full participation

### END OF MEETING EVALUATION

1. How safe did you feel at this meeting to share your thoughts, your questions, and your concerns?

   (very unsafe)          1          2          3          4          5 (very safe)

2. Describe what someone did at this meeting that helped you to feel safe.

3. How well did the group follow its norms?

   (poorly)          1          2          3          4          5 (very well)

4. How well did the conversation today focus on matters of importance?

   (poorly)          1          2          3          4          5 (very well)

5. How well did this meeting complicate your thinking or make you think differently about some aspect of the work?

   (poorly)          1          2          3          4          5 (very well)

6. Out of the following difficult conversation skills, place a check next to any that you practiced at today's meeting:

   Acknowledge feelings ☐

   Respond to criticism with curiosity ☐

   Disentangle impact from intention ☐

   Abandon blame ☐

   Balance advocacy with inquiry ☐

   Speak when you might rather remain silent ☐

   Listen! Don't just wait for your turn to talk ☐

   Allow for silences, and thinking, and letting things happen/emerge ☐

7. Closing thoughts or reflections?

*Source: Springfield Leadership Team Protocol* (Cambridge, MA: Massachusetts Education Partnership and Rennie Center for Education Research & Policy, 2015).

inquiry-based approach allows participants to create an atmosphere in which ideas flow freely, teams are encouraged to maximize the amount of inquiry that takes place during meetings, aiming to minimize advocacy. This framing foreshadows the key principles of the interest-based process discussed in chapter 4, which present a similar dichotomy between interests (inquiry-based) and proposals (advocacy-based).

### Strategy 5: Clearly Define Roles and Responsibilities

All too often team members rush to begin work, eager to start making progress on a defined goal, before taking time to understand the working styles and skill sets of the other team members. Teams that slow down and build a sense of trust and understanding prior to commencing work, lay a solid foundation for collaboration that encourages future success. Starting off with a strong sense of who is on the team and what skills and interests they have allows each team member to feel valued and encourages a sense of shared responsibility and ownership of the work. It also allows the team to actively recruit additional members if gaps in skills or positions are identified, a process that is more difficult once the team is well established.[27]

**FIGURE 3.3**    Inquiry versus advocacy

| Issue | Advocacy | Inquiry |
|---|---|---|
| Concept of decision making | A contest | Collaborative problem solving |
| Purpose of discussion | Persuasion and lobbying | Testing and evaluation |
| Participants' roles | Spokespeople | Critical thinkers |
| Patterns of behavior | Strive to persuade others; defend your positions; downplay weakness | Present balanced arguments; remain open to alternatives; accept constructive criticism |
| Minority views | Discouraged or dismissed | Cultivated and valued |
| Outcome | Winners and losers | Collective ownership |

During this period of team formation, members are advised to make clear any time constraints they may have, as well as to indicate the type of role they would like to assume on the team. A common problem in teams is having mismatched expectations, which can lead to assumptions that an individual is taking over the project and not being collaborative, or is skirting work and isn't invested. Starting with a clean slate by sharing expectations and roles can help avoid conflict in the long run. Additionally, it is expected that team structures will change over the life of the project.[28] Sometimes this may happen because of the demands of the project, while at other times it may be because of changes in district personnel or team member availability. Either way, teams will grow and evolve along with their work.

## FORMING TEAMS AND MANAGING CONFLICT IN FALL RIVER

The work going on in Fall River, Massachusetts, is an illustration of how to identify a problem and form a collaborative team to generate solutions.[29] Located in southeastern Massachusetts, the community of Fall River has a higher proportion of low-income and minority residents compared to the state. The medium household income is $33,763, less than 50 percent of the state average of $67,846. Educational attainment is also low, with 13.8 percent of residents above the age of twenty-five having received a bachelor's degree compared to the state average of 40 percent.[30] These demographics are also reflected in the students served by the Fall River Public School District. Of the 10,000 students in the district, more than two-thirds are considered high-needs due to disability, English language learner status, or economic disadvantage. Student outcomes on state accountability measures are also low; due to chronic underperformance the district is classified by the state as in need of intensive assistance.[31] To make matters worse, the school system and union had a historically contentious labor-management relationship; the last contract negotiation took almost two years—643 days—to reach agreement.

Given the urgent need for change and improvement, the superintendent and union president decided to try something different. In 2012, they entered into the District Capacity Project (DCP) with the goal of finding a way to work together productively to improve student outcomes. Initially, the union and district members of the DCP expressed differing views of the work and a lack of trust. As one member said, "The perception and reality is there was a lack of trust on both sides." While the two sides had different perspectives about the work, they were both committed to improving relations and saw the DCP as an opportunity to secure support.

After two months of meeting, members began to establish some basic ground rules around collaboration and narrowed in on the topic of developing professional learning communities in schools. The group developed a graphic representation of the focused project that illustrated how professional learning communities were embedded within the goal of increased student achievement (see figure 3.4).

While the initial work was very challenging, the group began to develop a trusting relationship. Said one member, "Agreeing on a collective project was our first challenge. We had to build that trust and put aside our egos and personal agendas." The group finally decided that a next step was to develop a survey that assessed the baseline school climate in each school. The plan was to use the results from the survey to help implement professional learning communities in schools. One member of the DCP team commented, "The initial survey is a great plan. At this point, we are just trying to get honest answers from teachers and staff about the climate and perceptions of the school."

The survey was jointly communicated by the union president and superintendent, but teachers were still worried about participating because the survey required a log-in. The DCP team worked to protect the teachers' anonymity by assigning everyone the same log-in. In the end, participation was significantly higher than in other similar climate surveys. With support from the union field rep, the principal and union building representatives were now able to sit down together and jointly discuss results—in

**FIGURE 3.4**   Fall River project

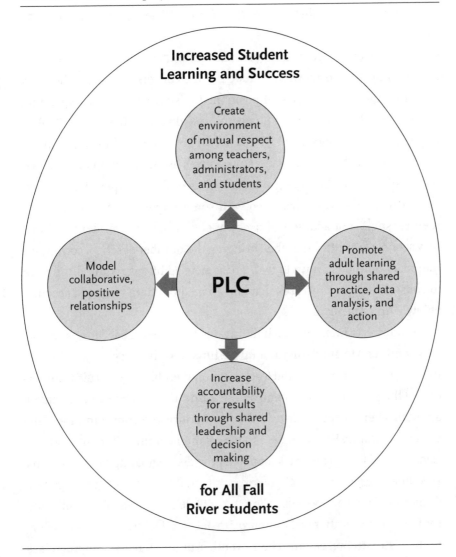

particular, strengths and weaknesses. The next step was to develop a work plan that could be operationalized through a formal Professional Learning Community (PLC). One union member of the team reflected on the initial process: "There is a long history of animosity, so the trust factor was a challenge at first. However, that disappeared relatively quickly as we began working together." A district member agreed: "They need us as much as we need them."

With a strong base of support, and assurance that the people most impacted by the project were included in the conversation early, the team went into the second year well positioned to start working on expanding the use and effectiveness of PLCs within the district.[32] But during its PLC implementation project, Fall River encountered both shifting team membership due to changes in leadership, as well as an evolution of roles and responsibilities as the work grew and changed. For example, after the first year of work, the team was faced with some important changes in team membership—the addition of a newly elected union president and one new school committee member, bringing the number of school committee members on the team up to two. These new additions required the team to consistently use processes that encouraged building trust and accountability within the team.

In addition to internal trust building, the team also needed to ensure that they continued to build trust among the three stakeholder groups (administration, school committee, and teacher union members), as the ultimate success of the project would depend on the team's ability to build and maintain support. Therefore, in year two, the team prioritized communication and capacity building. For example, as a part of their communication effort they established a formal feedback loop that provided regular updates to all three stakeholder groups. To encourage capacity building, the team engaged the Center for Collaborative Education to facilitate a training on best practices for PLCs that was attended by approximately 150 faculty (with every school in the district represented). The November professional development session allowed for faculty to become familiar with the practices that promote high-functioning PLCs, versed in the district's standardized PLC protocol, and able to move forward with PLC action planning. Shortly after the professional development session, with action plans in hand, the DCP team conducted a large feedback session in February on PLC implementation that was followed up by a survey and in-school observations to determine what additional supports would bolster PLC success.

In the third year, the team again encountered a shift. After having built the capacity of the PLCs to influence practice (through extensive professional development, action planning, and modeling), the team struggled to identify the roles that team members could play in supporting effective implementation. Although the team as currently configured could monitor the initiative, the work of sustaining PLCs would inevitably fall on building-level leaders. The team therefore changed its strategy and shifted the work to principals for the support and maintenance of PLCs in their buildings. In this new role, the team worked to establish differentiated supports and structures that could ensure that all schools are functioning as effective PLCs. An example of this effort can be seen in the team's creation of an online catalogue for PLC resources and demonstrations of best practice.

As seen in the Fall River case, it is very common for the design team to have to rely on other individuals for implementation and the long-term success of the project, so transparent communication is key. The surveys, presentations, and joint communication that the Fall River team did during the first and second years, are a nice example of building a solid platform of mutual investment and then shifting responsibility to those responsible for implementation. Inevitably, though, as team composition changes and people representing different stakeholders form new working relationships, there will be conflict. How else could *stakeholders explore their differences and construct solutions that are better than what they could have come up with on their own?*[33] To do so requires managing conflict effectively.

## BUMPS IN THE ROAD: SUSTAINING TEAMS THROUGH CONFLICT

A shared understanding of how to manage conflict is an often-overlooked aspect of effective teaming. Most teams think that if everyone works well together, there will not be any conflict. To the contrary, conflict is at the foundation of productive teams. As teaming expert Amy Edmondson writes, "Conflict among collaborators can feel like a failure, but differences in perspective are a core reason for teamwork in the first place, and resolving them effectively creates opportunities."[34] Teams that know how communicate and resolve disagreements are working well together; those that do not will find themselves either dissolving or falling back on traditional approaches to solution generation—narrowed focus, groupthink, and limited options—none of which encourage effective decision making on strategies that are evidence-based.

So, how do you get the most out of conflict, while still being able to work together? First, you must clearly understand when conflict promotes learning and when it prevents learning. For our purposes, we categorize conflict into two discrete categories: constructive conflict and destructive conflict.[35] Constructive conflicts are those disagreements that individuals or groups have over ideas. This type of conflict typically involves different ideas and solutions about how to move forward and is crucial to collective problem solving, conscious decision making, and long-term innovation. An example of a constructive conflict would be a district leader who is interested in exploring better curriculum development, while others would prefer to discuss the potential for common planning time, leading to more interdepartmental curricular opportunities.

Destructive conflict is different from constructive conflict in one crucial way: it is emotional and targets the individual rather than the idea. Destructive conflict can take the form of clashing personalities or strong-willed attacks. We have all been in situations where sides are being defended and it is no longer about the idea, but about winning. In these types of situations the likelihood for lingering resentment is high, and listening and learning from others is low.

The goal is to minimize destructive conflict, while increasing constructive conflict. To manage conflict, teams can follow the previously mentioned strategies—for example, create norms that explicitly state how communication will function within the team. This process of collectively creating norms can manage some conflict, but unless everyone agrees to the rules of engagement and is held accountable to them, the exercise will not effectively manage all "people problems" on the team. If a team is struggling with managing internal communication, it can be helpful for leaders to consider standardizing how arguments are framed, or it may be useful to have a third-party facilitator to act as a grounding agent, as providing a neutral perspective can greatly improve team dynamics and encourage mutual ownership.

With or without the help of a facilitator, teams can use the following five-step approach to effectively manage cognitive conflict and move towards issue resolution.

*Speak up and identify the issue.*[36]  It is important that the team members feel they have the space to express themselves and voice dissent freely. Creating an environment that is built on trust and encourages psychological safety ensures that individual voices will be taken into consideration. This is key, as "voice without consideration is often damaging; it leads to resentment and frustration rather than to acceptance."[37] Teams that function well encourage different ideas and opinions, and work hard to explore and understand how different people are conceptualizing the issue. This is a good starting point for constructive problem solving, if the issue is a priority to the team.

*Listen intently.* A core element of encouraging folks to speak up is making sure to listen and ask questions. Oftentimes, people are concerned with responding quickly and resolving conflict on the spot by promoting a hasty solution or defending whatever is already in force. Teams can benefit from taking a reflective rather than reactive approach to issues. Asking questions that elicit learning promotes understanding and reflection, which may not be a natural reaction, as many individuals are wired to respond to problems in a knee-jerk fashion. If this is the case, it can be helpful to either hire or develop a facilitator who can make sure discussions are learning-oriented and who encourages listening intently to the ideas and concerns of others.[38]

*Experiment.* Now is the time to think through potential solutions to the issue raised, while keeping in mind the core interests of the parties at the table. This process requires the team to move into a positive, creative, problem-solving mode—a mode that is inquiry-based rather than advocacy-based. This process also requires active listening, but it is not focused on understanding the issue, as in the previous step, but rather on generating as many options as possible.[39]

To aid teams in the process of generating solutions, it can be important to establish a brainstorming protocol that may include norms such as "no judgment or criticism," "wildness is welcome," "more ideas are better than few ideas," "combination and improvement is encouraged," "listen intently," and "keep a positive mind."[40]

So, what do teams do if there is silence and nobody is generating ideas? Or what if you can't get to more ideas because the focus is narrowed or certain team members feel that they already know the answer and effectively shut down other possibilities, balking at further analysis? Remember that stopping a brainstorm too early limits conversation and may leave you with a mediocre answer, so facilitators can choose to allow the group to reconvene once people have had a chance to think and come up with some ideas, or they can take a short break and try to cultivate other minority views. Either way, you need participation and you need generation to ensure involvement and buy-in, as well as to ensure that you have options to choose between.[41]

*Reflect.* With many potential solutions to the problem at hand, the team is faced with the next challenge of narrowing the change items down to one or a few solutions. Teams are encouraged to ask themselves the following three questions for each change idea:

- How responsive is this to the problem or issue at hand?
- How feasible is this?
- Would this solution if chosen be acceptable to all parties at the table, as well as to the broader stakeholder groups affected?

If a solution is not responsive, not feasible, or not acceptable, then it may not be the best solution to the problem and should likely be tabled, while others that are responsive, feasible, and acceptable can be kept as options.

*Integrate.* Now that the team understands the challenge, each member's interest in its resolution, and some possible or acceptable solutions, it is time to resolve the issue. There are two ways to come to a resolution, either through a vote or through consensus. At first glance voting seems like the quicker, easier way of doing business, as it is often how we make decisions and is well understood. Consensus, on the other hand, appears messy and long, lacking a way to move forward unless everyone loves the solution, which may mean nothing gets done. When you look a bit closer, though, there are also some considerable flaws with voting—primarily, that it creates a dichotomy of winners and losers. Those whose voices are outnumbered during a vote will likely have decreased commitment to the work, which may hurt the long-term potential of the decision. To avoid the pitfalls of both these approaches—voting and consensus—we suggest that teams use a consensus-based model, but that they avoid the messiness by clearly defining consensus so that the work can still get done with everyone on board. Here is one definition of consensus that you may choose to use:

> All members agree upon a single alternative, and each group member can honestly say: I believe that you understand my point of view and I understand yours. Whether or not this is my first choice for a decision, I will support it because 1) it was reached fairly and openly, and 2) it is the best solution for us at this time.[42]

Using this definition suggests that consensus doesn't mean we all got our way and our preferred solution or program won. It instead states that the process we followed was agreed to and was done with fidelity, and that this solution is seen as the best at this time.

### The Role of Facilitators

A facilitator can be a valuable asset to a team as its members begin to work together, especially when that team is diverse and has many different approaches to problem solving. Facilitators can help manage group dynamics with an eye toward building the team's capacity to carry the work forward, eventually without them. Survey data gathered from teams involved in the District Capacity Project found facilitators to be a critical component of success. The teams highly valued the facilitators' support, as shown by the fact that all of the teams agreed that the facilitator provided helpful insight to their team processes, and 98 percent reported that the facilitator effectively promoted collaboration. Of course, not all facilitators are the same, and it takes skill to manage a team of diverse stakeholders. We have found the following key roles to be effective for facilitators:

- Hold stakeholders accountable by reminding the team of its ground rules
- Keep collaboration moving forward by establishing protocols for identifying and resolving issues
- Serve as an outlet when conversations break down
- Provide training and coaching to help the team master collaboration skills and practices

A facilitator who understands his or her role in the light of these four functions can avoid overstepping and being viewed as favoring one stakeholder's perspectives over another's.

## CONCLUSION

The preceding evidence is clear: improvement is bolstered through the design and effective implementation of processes that enhance collaboration. Additionally, creating an environment where collaborators feel psychologically safe is a key ingredient to creating teams that continuously learn and that adapt quickly to new information. LMC collaborative teams should prioritize five key strategies as they begin working together: establish a clear and ambitious purpose that is a priority; be thoughtful when creating or expanding the team; allow space to team; clearly define the roles and responsibilities of team members; and establish team norms. When conflict emerges, which it will, follow the steps outlined to manage it productively. Finally, the team may benefit from a facilitator, as long as he or she understands his or her role.

The real work begins once the team is formed. In the next chapter we discuss the complexities of getting a diverse group of stakeholders to work together on a common project. Even after following the best practices for team formation and using a process to manage conflict, LMC collaboration is challenging. To sustain work and make the team more effective, we suggest using an interest-based process for problem-solving. Discussed in detail in chapter 4, the interest-based process deals exclusively with the interests, not positions, of stakeholders. In doing so, the process identifies common interests across stakeholders that can be used to drive change in a system.

# Appendix (Chapter 3)

## Teaming Resources

Tool 1: **Learning Organization Survey** This survey was developed by
Amy Edmondson, David Garvin, and Francesca Gino at Harvard
University. It can be used to analyze the extent to which your unit
is functioning as a learning organization. This free survey can also
help you understand the factors that are affecting your ability to be a
learning organization. For a complete tool, as well as scoring, visit,
https://hbs.qualtrics.com/jfe/form/SV_b7rYZGRxuMEyHRz.

Tool 2: **Understanding the Challenge** This tool was designed by the
Massachusetts Education Partnership and is meant to provide both
a macro and micro picture of one problem the team is hoping to
address. To do this, teams are asked to map out the nature of the
challenge or problem that they are tackling, identify an area of key
focus, and zero in on their preferred approach for addressing the
problem. This document is meant to help teams discuss the problem and solution more fully, aiding in the onboarding of new team
members and old alike. This exercise also provides a nice segue
to project planning. For the complete tool, see renniecenter.org/
IETresources.

Tool 3: **Team Capacity Review** This two-page survey was developed
by the Massachusetts Education Partnership to provide teams
and facilitators with data about their team in the areas of processes and operations; teaming and relationship building; capacity,

sustainability, and adaptability; communication; and project management and implementation. This tool is intended to give both
teams and facilitators the opportunity to reflect on many important
components related to carrying out the work of their projects as well
as teaming. It also gives teams and facilitators a better understanding of the team's areas of strength and areas in need of improvement. This document should be thought of as a jumping-off point
for the work ahead. For the complete tool, see renniecenter.org/
IETresources.

*Tool 4: Charrette for Group Learning* This is a brainstorming approach
where a group or individual presents a scenario with a focused
problem of practice to another (listening) group. After sufficient
time has been allowed for both the presentation of facts and clarify-
ing questions, the listening group is asked to discuss the problem
and generate solutions, while the presenters take notes. The presenters then have a chance to summarize the key takeaways they
heard. The protocol can be found at the National School Reform
Faculty, http://www.nsrfharmony.org/system/files/protocols/char-
rette_o.pdf.

*Tool 5: Belbin's Framework* Belbin's Framework can be used when initially forming a team, or once a team has been formed, to assess
people's interest and ability to fulfill certain roles. This model places
people into three categories, each of which is helpful to team success: action-oriented roles, people-oriented roles, and cerebral roles
There are nine distinct interrelated team roles that contribute to
successful team efforts: shaper, implementer, completer/finisher,
coordinator, team worker, resource investigator, creator/inventor,
monitor/evaluator, and the specialist.

*Tool 6: Fishbone diagram* This tool is used for a team to implement a
causal analysis. To complete a fishbone diagram, teams agree on a
problem (or effect), which is written down, ostensibly, at the fish's
head. Problem statements should be as specific as possible and not

framed as solutions that have yet to be addressed (e.g., "We need to provide more professional development to teachers"). Teams then brainstorm and agree on broad categories that account for the major causes of the identified problem. Additional brainstorming identifies subcauses within each category, developing a skeletal structure where primary categories and subcauses are linked. In the brainstorming process, all ideas are considered valid and suggested causes may be placed under multiple categories. A protocol can be found at the Innovation Center, http://www.theinnovation-center.org/.

**CHAPTER 4**

# Interest-Based Process

## BUILDING TRUST AND MANAGING CONFLICT

WHEN AN LMC TEAM BEGINS ITS WORK, there is bound to be a difference of opinions about how to solve a particular problem. For union leaders, the key to improving student achievement in the district might be giving teachers more autonomy in the classroom or enhanced professional learning opportunities. On the management side, district administrators may call for greater professional accountability or improved evaluation processes. Community stakeholders may bring an entirely different set of solutions to the table that could include improved communication, renovated school facilities, or hiring teachers who reflect the backgrounds of children in the community.

When labor, management, and community stakeholders begin the team process, they may think of going into battle, armed with their inflexible perspective and solution. With this frame in mind, discussion on the team may follow a familiar scenario. One side proposes its solution, usually one that may not be acceptable (or even possible) to the others, and the process of negotiating begins. Each side digs in, clinging to its solution with defensive reasoning, not allowing other solutions in for fear that it will weaken their position. This adherence to a rigid position takes the focus off solving the problem and puts it instead on a much more personal level, turning a process problem into a people problem. As in most battles, only the fittest arguments survive, and by the end, one side has "won" at the expense of the others.[1]

This snapshot of negotiations embodies a positional or distributive approach to bargaining in which stakeholders position themselves for battle with the assumption that there are finite resources and that each solution must be argued using a zero-sum approach.[2] Although there are some issues that are distributive in nature, such as professional development requirements or planning time, changing the lens by which stakeholders view LMC collaboration can lead parties toward an approach that allows for the pursuit of mutual benefits and that is problem-solving rather than problem-producing.

By taking a problem-solving approach, stakeholders are able to prioritize resolving issues by considering many possible options—unbounded solution generation—and then limiting the pool of options by only focusing on those solutions that are both realistic and meet all parties' interests. This comes in contrast with a positional approach, which aims to resolve differences by negotiating within a bounded set of positions, in which the solution is constrained by the fact that parties do not engage in problem solving together.

This chapter outlines a problem-solving approach known as interest-based process (IBP). Many are familiar with the concept of interest-based bargaining, which is a strategy used for contract negotiations. Although the literature drawn upon in the chapter, as well as the process elements outlined, come from interest-based bargaining, we have reframed the language and expanded some of the strategies to ensure that the approach can be used at and beyond the bargaining table, as a conflict resolution strategy. Throughout the chapter, we advocate for the use of IBP as a way for diverse stakeholders to explore issues, understand each other's perspectives, brainstorm possible resolutions, and jointly agree to a solution that can be implemented together.

To anyone reading this who has been involved in collective bargaining, the interest-based approach we describe here may sound utopian. Yet evidence from the field suggests that it can in fact be done, and numerous cases have documented the benefits of a more collaborative approach. Using an interest-based process has been shown to produce significant time-saving benefits, create a foundation that allows for an increase in key "transformational" outcomes (such as increased workplace flexibility and increased job security), and reduce the escalation of grievances and other costly disputes.[3]

In this chapter we will first describe how taking an interest-based approach changes the process of potentially contentious discussions, including an explanation of the key structural differences between traditional and interest-based approaches. After a brief overview of the historical use of the interest-based process, as seen through the lens of collective bargaining, along with an exploration of trends in current practice, we will go on to describe the process step by step, highlighting select tools that districts can use to support the approach. Embedded in our description of the process will be a first-hand account of the interest-based approach through the eyes of education leaders in Rockford County Public Schools.

## A New Lens: Structural and Procedural Differences

The interest-based process is most often associated with and used in formal contract negotiations.[4] As defined by Kaboolian and Sutherland,[5] interest-based process is an approach to negotiations that focuses on the parties' shared interests and allows for the identification of multiple ways to satisfy interests and solve problems creatively. In this approach both relationships and outcomes are prioritized, with the hope of maximizing gains for all parties. Although for simplicity's sake IBP is often placed in opposition to traditional bargaining, these approaches are not completely separate. Instead, they should be thought of as part of a larger continuum of bargaining behaviors, with traditional bargaining on one end and collaborative techniques like IBP on the other.[6] This allows for fluidity in approach, as most negotiations encompass a variety of bargaining behaviors and structures.[7] Given that these approaches are at opposite ends of the spectrum, both the structure and process of negotiations can appear significantly different.

An IBP approach, which aims to maximize outcomes and to prioritize relationships, promotes structures meant to build and expand trust. One such example is the decentralized nature of communication in IBP, as compared to traditional bargaining. In IBP, when stakeholders come together, there is no elected spokesperson or negotiator for the representative organization. Because communication isn't streamlined through an elected or appointed spokesperson, there also is not as great a need for side caucusing. When used in an IBP, side caucusing has more restricted goals: getting everyone caught up on the matters being discussed at side tables; allowing each side to reflect on, and become comfortable with, what is being said at the main table (most prevalent at the beginning or end of negotiations); and facilitating intraparty bargaining when distributive issues are being negotiated.[8] The reason for the minimalist nature of side caucusing during IBP is that parties are encouraged to work together as much as possible, building trust so that discussing things away from the main table is not necessary. It is also the case that when overly utilized, side caucuses elicit a suspicion that information is not being shared, or that people are plotting among themselves, neither of which is conducive to collaborative problem solving.[9]

Since all team members are encouraged to speak freely, ask questions, and brainstorm solutions together, facilitators (either internal or external) are often seen as a key structural element of IBP and are there to encourage participation among all team members in problem solving.[10] In addition, facilitators often play a role in both skill and knowledge generation. As outlined by Macneil and Bray, facilitators have been shown to be involved in each of the following five areas: building motivation among parties to jointly resolve differences; generating knowledge of IBP practices among the team, as well as helping parties collect the needed data to understand the issues at hand; developing the parties' communication and listening skills; defining roles and understanding the relationships in the group to aid in communication and management of problems; and building an environment that encourages trust and transparency.[11] Training in IBP through an external facilitator is common. There is little research on the differences between internal or external facilitation; however, anecdotal evidence suggests that many districts feel more comfortable with the process when using external facilitators as a guide during their first time using IBP for negotiations.[12]

Beyond the facilitator, IBP is based in collaborative problem solving, a process that is bolstered by transparent information sharing during negotiations. A strong emphasis is placed on working together to gather data that can help to clarify the issues and generate potential solutions. As John Bukey, an education law attorney in Sacramento suggests, IBP changes the expectation of participants. "The collaborative process precludes frivolous demands and forces the parties to 'put their cards on the table.'"[13] They are expected to think about what they are doing and what is underlying their requests, in order to begin to resolve problems together. To aid in information gathering, multi-stakeholder subcommittees are often utilized and preside over certain issues.[14] Such subcommittees often include experts from the district or community, individuals who would normally not be included on the team. This expansion of the team is another difference between a traditional approach and IBP, as there is no restriction on the number of people included. Subcommittees allow team members to focus on select issues outside of the main table, giving them space to gather and analyze data and solve problems creatively with a smaller group of people and with diverse individuals who may offer unique and important perspectives on the matter at hand. It also means that not everything needs to be discussed by everyone, decreasing time overall, but increasing the time spent by select individuals on discrete issues.

Lastly, IBP differs significantly from the traditional approach in process. From its start, traditional negotiations focus on two opposing positions. In IBP, the parties first work to develop problem statements, and all parties focus on their shared interests behind the problem, working together toward resolution. As described in the classic IBP text *Getting to Yes*, the differences between interests and positions is significant. Positions are something you have decided upon. Interests are what caused you to so decide.[15] This difference is what allows for collaborative problem solving to take root. To better understand the difference between interests and positions, an excerpt from a concept exercise developed by Mary Ellen Shea is included here (see figure 4.1). This exercise is meant to help clarify interests, positions, and perceptions.[16]

## A Brief History of the Interest-Based Process

The principles of IBP can be traced back to three significant sources, starting with the sociologist Mary Parker Follett, one of the foremost management scholars of the early twentieth century. With scientific management at its peak, Parker Follett was writing and lecturing on the power of shared decision making and the "integration of interests as a means of conflict management," a more humanistic approach.[17] During a series of lectures given in 1933 to the Department of Business Administration at the London School of Economics, Parker Follett commented on conflict management, stating:

> In dominating, only one [side] gets what it wants; in compromise neither side gets what it wants . . . Is there any other way of dealing with difference? There is a way beginning now to be recognized at least and sometimes followed, the way of integration . . . The extraordinarily interesting thing about this is that the third way means progress. In domination, you stay where you are. In compromise likewise you deal with no new values. By integration something new has emerged, the third way, something beyond the either-or.[18]

This insight proved foundational, and spurred other organizational scholars to consider alternative approaches to negotiations that focused more on resolving conflict without domination or compromise. Following her

**FIGURE 4.1**   Concept exercise in classifying interests and positions

---

**Position:**     A party's demand for a particular outcome.

**Interest:**     The concern underlying a party's position.

**Perception:**   An untested belief or assumption held by a party.

**Manager:**    "If the Providence Pioneers are going to beat the Hartford Hustlers, we gotta get some left-handed pitching."

**Owner:**    "If you want pitching, get a right-hander. Lefties get murdered in Pioneer Stadium."

**Manager:**    "Remember, we play half our games on the road. And we need a southpaw against the Hustlers' left-handed power."

**Owner:**    "Who do you have in mind?"

**Manager:**    "Phoebe Flutterball. She's 34 but still an amazing pitcher. Last year she had the fourth-best earned run average in the league. She's not very well known only because she plays for the last place Denver Dames."

**Owner:**    "Yeah, but her agent is asking for $600,000 a year. For a little more we could sign Liz Lightning. She can throw that baby in at over 80 mph. She packs in the fans too: they love her."

**Manager:**    "Well, I don't know. She walks too many batters and I hear she's a complainer. Phoebe's a team player."

**Owner:**    "Maybe the best thing is to put the money into the farm club. That would increase the long-run value of the ball club and give us some good inexpensive, younger players *(a better investment of my shares!)*."

**Manager:**    "Improving the farm team is a good idea, but we need another pitcher now. A good farm system won't help is this year. Frankly, I'm sick of being called a loser and getting slammed by the reporters *(especially since I need to renegotiate my contract at the end of the year!)*."

**Owner:**    "I'd like to win too, but I can't spend unlimited amounts of money. I'm responsible to the Board of Directors. I only own 15% of the team. They won't go for a deal where the costs are high and the payback is not certain."

Classify each statement below as a position, interest, or perception.

1. "I won't pay over $400,000 a year for a pitcher."
2. "Left-handed pitchers are usually ineffective in Pioneer Stadium."
3. "$500,000 is too much to pay for a left-handed pitcher."
4. "I'd like to have a good pitching staff."
5. "We should sign Liz Lightening immediately."
6. "I wish the sports writers gave me more respect."
7. "The Board of Directors wouldn't like my spending $600,000 for Phoebe Flutterball."

---

work, in 1965 Richard Walton and Robert McKersie published *A Behavioral Theory of Labor Negotiations.* Although heavily cited in contemporary literature, at the time of publication interest in approaching bargaining using collaboration or integrating interests was not mainstream. For example, as Jerome Barrett notes, "When the Federal Mediation and Conciliation Service (FMCS)[19] used the book to train new mediators in 1975, it was because of the many ways that it explained the adversarial dynamics of collective bargaining."[20] It was not for its unique approach to integration or any exploration of "the third way."

It wasn't until 1981, nearly sixty years after Parker Follett had explained a new approach, that it gained traction and was popularized by Roger Fisher and William Ury in their classic text, *Getting to Yes.* Although greeted with skepticism, and confronting a harsh climate for labor unions under the Reagan administration, Fisher and Ury's text, derived from processes developed by the Harvard Negotiations Project, provided a clear foundation for the negotiating techniques we now call interest-based bargaining.[21]

Since its popularization, IBP has gained significant traction and has become a fairly well known alternative to traditional, positional approaches. Although dated by now, the data collected by FMCS between 1996 and 2001 shows the use of IBP in approximately 5.44 percent of negotiations (over 1,500 negotiations during the five-year period).[22] Slightly more recently, a national survey conducted in 2004 revealed that in collective bargaining states where FMCS provides services, between 70 and 80 percent of negotiators reported experience with IBP and between 15 and 30 percent of private sector negotiators reported its use.[23] These data suggest that although still not the dominant approach, IBP is being used across sectors and that most negotiators, at least at FMCS, have had experience with the approach.

While there is no comprehensive state-level analysis of IBP in the education sector, several states have collected data indicating an increase in the awareness and use of IBP. In 2014 an analysis of public-sector education negotiations was conducted in Massachusetts. Through a series of state-level surveys of school committees, superintendents, and union presidents, Kochan and others found that between 2011 and 2014 there was a 6 percent increase in the number of respondents who see collective bargaining as a means of improving school performance, with nearly 60 percent of respondents in 2014 rating their negotiations as collaborative.[24] In Oregon, a survey conducted between 1994 and 2000 by the Oregon School Boards Association showed an 11 percent increase in the number of districts using alternative strategies for their negotiations, indicating that between 44 and 47 percent of Oregon's districts were engaged in IBP or similar approaches during that period.[25] Although data suggests an uptick in use, the research is restricted by a lack of data collection, limiting our understanding of the number of negotiations that use IBP.

## INTEREST-BASED PROCESS: A WALK THROUGH THE STEPS

To avoid challenges associated with the search for a single answer from one stakeholder group, we encourage LMC teams to use the five steps in the interest-based process. The first two steps are for each stakeholder group to determine what issues it wishes to resolve during the team process, and to share its perspective on each of the selected items. Then all parties collectively generate a list of interests, or values, undergirding each issue, brainstorm options for resolution that can then be evaluated, and reach consensus on a solution to each case. Below we will go through each step and expand upon the process, while giving tips that can help parties implement the process effectively. Remember to keep in mind the basic principles of IBP as you progress through the chapter. Most of the principles listed in figure 4.2 were included in the section on structural and procedural differences, while a few may be new to you. This list of principles is a nice reminder of what the IBP process is, and we encourage you to use it as a tool to ground conversations.

**FIGURE 4.2** IBP principles

---

- Participation by labor, management, and community is VOLUNTARY.
- The parties and each negotiator/team member/facilitator make a COMMITMENT to engage in the interest-based process.
- All parties contribute to respectful and productive meetings by their commitment to consistent ATTENDANCE AND PARTICIPATION.
- All parties contribute to respectful and productive meetings by their commitment to BEHAVIOR that supports effective communication and interest-based decision making.
- COMMUNICATION between the parties is enhanced when they meet face to face and all members participate.
- How the parties will handle COMMUNICATIONS with constituents and with the public, is agreed in advance.
- Mutual gains are possible when the parties explore and understand both their INTERESTS.
- A collaborative, PROBLEM-SOLVING approach to issues leads to better agreements.
- INFORMATION that is necessary to the process is mutually determined, gathered, shared, and made available as quickly as possible.
- CONSENSUS decision making assures full support for the outcome.
- Agreement about HOW TO SEPARATE from IBP establishes trust in the process.
- LOGISTICS are arranged and agreed to in advance. All aspects of the process are considered, including who will participate, the schedule of meetings, whether to use a facilitator, record keeping, and how decisions will be made.

---

Please note that the description of IBP below is an overview and is meant to describe the process, providing a sampling of tools while at the same time highlighting accounts from the field. Interview excerpts from education leaders in Rockford Public Schools in Rockford, Illinois, will be used to ground the process.

Rockford Public Schools is one of the largest school districts in Illinois, serving 28,000 students and employing approximately 4,700 individuals. The district engaged in IBP for contract negotiations in 2015, crediting their collaborative bargaining success both to their adherence to the process and to the training and facilitation support they received from the Consortium for Educational Change and the Illinois Education Association.

*Step 1: Determine the issues.* The first step in IBP is for each party to sit down and think about what issues, or problems, they want to resolve through the team. This step may have been partly accomplished through the needs assessment process described in chapter 2. However, when using the IBP on an LMC team it is always good practice to have every stakeholder explicitly articulate what problem they are trying to solve, no matter what has been identified in the needs assessment. This process is different from generating a list of positions, in that it attempts to clearly identify the problem, rather than resolve it. Resolution will come, but it will be accomplished together and be agreeable to all parties—an integrated solution.

During the process, stakeholders are encouraged to involve constituents in the framing of the issues. This can be a more intensive process than creating goals or a wish list of wants, as it involves reshaping the conversation to focus on the things that need to be changed. Surveying constituents can be a good way of gathering data on the matters that are of most importance. When creating surveys we recommend that careful attention be paid to the wording of the tool, with a particular focus on ensuring that responses are problem-oriented. But what if you distribute the survey and get lots of responses, realizing only then that many of the responses focus on solutions! Not to worry. You can use the information gathered to write up the core issues and interests that you think are underlying the solutions offered.[26] To ensure that those you represent know these issues, and to avoid having them get too attached to their solutions, be sure to feed the core issues and interests back to them as the platform for the teamwork.

Although surveys are a great tool for generating a large amount of feedback to base negotiations on, surveys tend to elicit responses that are more localized; therefore, they are not as good at generating long-range goals, or focusing on strategic challenges that extend well beyond the present. If you are interested in understanding the broader themes, a complementary approach may be useful. One such approach is to host a series of focus groups where the entire LMC team can engage select representatives in a session focused on long-range goals, while at the same time discussing potential challenges or barriers to their achievement. Solidifying your broader agenda prior to meeting can protect you from agreeing to resolutions now that create barriers to the group's interests in the future.[27]

As experienced by Rockford Public Schools, both surveys and focus groups were cited as key to flushing out the issues. In the words of Paul Goddard, vice president of the Rockford Education Association, "With the new focus on developing narratives, instead of positions and demands, the team was forced to dig hard and find out the explanations for the priorities that the teachers identified. It really forced us to get to the why, instead of jumping to solutions." An example of this process was seen when the REA probed deeper into teachers' concerns about school facilities. When asked for specifics, many teachers said that they felt unable to influence seemingly simple things about their work environment, including the temperature of classrooms or whether their classroom had blinds. With adequate time to understand the narrative and ask about why this was the case, the issue became clearer. They realized that the person receiving facility's complaints had numerous other responsibilities that were of higher priority. With the issue clearly defined, solutions were much easier to come by, and the likelihood of resolution became more realistic.

*Step 2: Share your perspective.* Now that the stakeholders have engaged in gathering their issues, you are ready to engage further in the teamwork.[28] Each stakeholder should begin with stating "opening remarks," which are the big-picture version of the concerns held by each side. The opening remarks tell the story of what happened, who was involved, and what effect it is having.

It is important to note that at this point, all sharing is fairly high level, because the goal is to air the issues in an effort to prioritize and set a schedule for resolution. This process can take on a "cathartic" feel, as described by the president of the Rockford Education Association, Dawn Granath: "It made us realize that both sides had done some things that they shouldn't have. Honest reactions showed, though, that we wanted to change and make things better."

After team members have identified, shared, and highlighted the stories that surround each issue, there are a few different ways to start the process of working together to identify priorities and set an agenda. One way is to create a package or bundle of issues that can be discussed at the same time. If there are many bundled issues, teams may choose to designate subgroups or side tables to deal with select problems; or, if the issues are so vast they appear overwhelming, teams can elect to set a limit to the number of matters they will deal with. Although both the union and management of Rockford Public Schools had agreed to a set number of categories that each side would present, many large issues—such as co-curricular differentials, challenges in retaining new teachers in hard-to-fill positions and schools, and retirement incentives—arose that seemed too big to resolve over the course of six months. So instead of trying to address everything, both teams decided to think of bargaining as an ongoing continuum of problem solving that would need to extend beyond the six-month negotiation timeline. Rockford superintendent Dr. Ehren Jarrett explained, "It was an epiphany . . . it took the pressure off because we didn't have to solve every issue. We gave ourselves permission to make progress on select issues and we worked out a process to work towards a resolution on the other issues."

Even though there was an acceptance among the team that certain matters would have to be resolved later, this wasn't always comfortable. First, given the number of issues to work through, it was difficult to figure out which ones to prioritize, and it took a while for all parties to agree on which ones needed immediate resolution. Additionally, some team members expressed nervousness that those problems that were not prioritized would in effect be "kicked down the road" and would remain unresolved.

After prioritizing the issues, depending on time constraints, teams may choose to redevelop the problem statements, especially for any bundled issues. This collaborative exercise can help to ensure that neither party feels that only the other side is represented in the issue statement.[29] This is also a good time to determine key logistics, such as scheduling and data collection. Dr. Michael Gaffney, a labor relations expert and long-time facilitator of conflict resolution, advises that teams "allow three to four hours per issue; roughly two to three issues per eight-hour day. Add to this one day for preliminaries and one to two days for wrapping up."[30] He also advises that teams make sure that distributive issues are not left until the end, as these often require teams to research and determine objective standards that help with their resolution. Placing these somewhere in the middle of the timetable is ideal.[31] Lastly, be sure not to overlook your data needs. If you do a quick scan of the issues now and map out a strategy for getting the data you need, assigning joint data collection to select individuals, you avoid delays down the road caused by gaps in knowledge.

*Step 3: Generate a list of interests, or values, undergirding the issue.* Now that you have reconvened around one issue, it can be beneficial for the team to recap its history, or to share data gathered between meetings. This process creates a level platform for the next phase in the interest-based process: unpacking your interests. Remember that interests are the concerns or values you hold related to the issue that you don't want overlooked, so be thorough. As a means of team integration, try to list your interests back and forth—that way you don't end up with two seemingly separate lists of interests. Rotating interest statements also helps people not to get attached to their side's interests only.

Since this is a group problem-solving exercise, common interests are highlighted, and all options generated in the next step are meant to address these common interests. "How we solve common interests was on everyone's mind," said Rockford School Board member Timothy Rollins. Conversations around kindergarten class size, one of the largest issues for the REA, proved to be great examples of group problem solving, since union and administration both agreed that reducing class size would be beneficial (shared common interest) and agreed to work together to figure out where the money could come from. Of course conversation surround-ing various issues, including kindergarten class size, weren't without slip-ups, and as the process moved along some power interactions took place between members of the same organization. For example, Rollins noted there were cases "when a REA [Rockford Education Association] member would say 'That's *your* interest,' and another REA member would say—in correction—'No, that is *our* interest.'"

To ensure that all parties are understanding each other's interests, the process of paraphrasing—proof of active listening—forces any miscom-munication to be clarified on the spot.[32] Repeating does not mean that you share the thought or feeling, but instead is an act to ensure that communica-tion is clear. This should be stated at the outset, as sometimes paraphrasing can be taken as consent or agreement with, rather than clarification of, an opinion. This process can be aided by IBP training programs that dedicate a portion of time to effective strategies for communicating clearly.

*Step 4: Brainstorm options for issue resolution that can then be evaluated.* Moving on from collective interests, the team is now challenged to develop options that address those interests and ultimately resolve the problem. Option generation should be thought of as a brainstorming exercise. The process of creating is hindered by judgment, so teams are encouraged to "separate the process of thinking up possible decisions from the process of selecting among them. Invent first, decide later."[33] Some simple ground rules for brainstorming can be adopted to provide a platform for constructive idea generation. Bulleted below are sample ground rules from the Massachusetts Education Partnership's *All About Brainstorming*, which include:

- No criticism, no evaluation, no discussion of ideas.
- There are no stupid ideas. The wilder the better.
- All ideas are recorded.
- Piggybacking is encouraged: combining, modifying, expanding oth-ers' ideas. Invent before you judge: no critique yet!

- Go for quantity: more ideas, more variety.
- Record the contribution, not the contributor.
- Separate inventing from commitment.
- Every idea is recorded for all to see.
- Ask questions for clarity only; explanations later.
- Keep going until all options have been exhausted![34]

There is a tendency to engage in brainstorming and generate lots of options that teams then want to share with their constituents. This is not recommended! The reason is because you have not yet evaluated the options, and there may be many that are not feasible, or do not satisfy your mutual interests. Given that many constituents are not physically at the table for bargaining, but instead have an acting representative, the likelihood of mis-interpretation is high, and options may be thought of not as possibilities but as the things you have decided on or that are likely to happen. If you want to share something, the list of shared interests is a better choice and is less likely to be misinterpreted.[35] To organize the issue, interests, and options, a tracking sheet like the one developed by the Massachusetts Education Partnership can be useful (see figure 4.3)

Once you have exhausted all options, the next step is to evaluate them. Three criteria can be used to evaluate options. First, is the solution respon-sive to the problem we are trying to address? Second, is it feasible? And lastly, is the solution acceptable to all parties and does it respect our shared interests? If the solution meets all three criteria, then it may be the answer to the problem, moving the team into the next and final stage of the pro-cess—resolution by consensus.

*Step 5: Reach consensus on a solution to each issue.* Similar to the conflict man-agement approach described in chapter 3, IBP decisions are made by con-sensus, which involves getting full group support for the solution at hand. Given the extensiveness of collaboration during teamwork or negotiations, consensus should not be hard to achieve and should be clearly defined prior

**FIGURE 4.3**  Issue tracking sheet

| Issue | Interests | Options | OPTIONS Evaluated | STILL NEED ... | STATUS |
|---|---|---|---|---|---|
| *diagnose/ analyze* | *discussion, sharing* | *brainstorming* | *criteria* | | |
| Framed and understood | Explored and understood | Thoroughly explored | Responsive? Feasible? Acceptable? | Awaiting: (more data, discussion, related issue) | Approaching resolution? |
| | | | | | |
| | | | | | |
| | | | | | |
| | | | | | |
| | | | | | |
| | | | | | |
| | | | | | |
| | | | | | |

to engaging in the IBP process (usually in the team's ground rules). A commonly held definition of consensus is when each person is at least 70 percent comfortable with the decision and 100 percent willing to support it. Making decisions by consensus supports collaboration by ensuring that all team members are in agreement that they can live with the decision at hand

and that this decision is the best for the group at this time. It also precludes statements like "I didn't vote for that" or "That was their decision." When consensus is reached on a solution to a problem, the impact on team members is tangible. As Rockford Superintendent Jarrett described, "When you converge the willingness of three groups—through training, facilitation, and a collaborative mindset—there is an amplification that occurs and a newfound efficiency to the way you solve problems together."

## IBP Beyond the Team and Bargaining Table

There are some issues that require multiyear efforts to resolve or that may be perennial to improving student learning. The LMC team should recognize those long-term concerns and commit to extending their work throughout the community. Facing precisely this case, Rockford Public Schools decided to form joint subcommittees to resolve ongoing issues that went beyond the scope of the contract. The choice to use subcommittees provided the team not only more time, but also an opportunity to include more people in decisions—spreading an interest-based culture throughout the system.

Seven subcommittees, each of which included at least two bargaining team members, were established after contract ratification. These committees focused on different issue areas, including differentials, hard-to-fill positions and schools, compensation, collaboration, staffing structures, elementary report cards, and school councilor job descriptions. Placing individuals who had been through IBP training on each team ensured that the teams would function using collaborative problem-solving processes and principles. Additionally, subcommittees that were deemed to be at high risk for resorting to a positional approach—those dealing with compensation and staffing structures—used external facilitators. Overall, eighty representatives from across the district were chosen jointly to fill the subcommittees, representing teachers, principals, central office administrators and support staff. To ensure accountability, each group was required to report their progress quarterly to the standing district negotiation's team. The goal from the beginning was to have the majority of issues resolved before the next negotiation's cycle, with a few remaining but queued for resolution.

Although things were slow at first, with many meetings dedicated to building capacity and getting new members situated, by the end of the year things started to coalesce. A few issues, including those around professional development and compensation had been resolved, while progress on the remaining ones was well under way. Superintendent Jarrett commented that the teams learned some important lessons this past year, including the importance of 1) prioritizing consistent subcommittee structures and meetings schedules to help the team lay a solid foundation; 2) encouraging principal involvement, especially for issues that involve building level changes; and 3) establishing work plans and timelines to aid team progress and decision making. According to Jarrett, with the IBP framework in place, subcommittees were creating an environment that encouraged "more innovation and creative thinking. We are continuing to build our capacity to, in the words of Michael Fullan, 'walk the talk.'"

## CONCLUSION

The interest-based process requires a shift in how stakeholders perceive the problems they are trying to solve. Specifically, IBP requires them to see teamwork as a chance to solve problems together and focus on their shared interest, improving teaching and learning for all students. By taking an interest-based approach, team members generate many solutions, encourage creativity, and adopt resolutions by consensus, increasing the likelihood of effective implementation.

Using an interest-based approach comes with some key structural differences as compared to a more traditional approach. Some of the structures that can support an interest-based approach include: decentralized communication in which all are encouraged to speak; limited use of side caucuses in favor of an expanded use of joint subcommittees; facilitators that aid the process instead of mediators; transparent information sharing; and a focus on interests rather than positions.

With an understanding of the different structural elements, it is also important that teams use the IBP effectively. IBP starts with each stakeholder determining what issue it wishes to resolve and then sharing their perspective on it. As seen in the case of Rockford Public Schools, this process can help to clarify the problem and identify key interests. It can also be cathartic for the group to share stories about festering problems, bringing about joint understanding with the hope for future resolution. Building a platform of understanding is integral to the next step in the interest-based process, which involves collectively generating a list of interests that undergird each issue and brainstorming options for resolution. With evaluation and consensus coming last, the process is meant to be an exercise in group problem-solving where everyone is included and where all have an opportunity to voice dissent, but where consensus is achieved when everyone on the bargaining team is at least 70 percent comfortable with the decision and 100 percent willing to support it.

Once a solution is reached, we encourage stakeholders to create structures that can resolve ongoing issues and that act to encourage communication. Forming joint subcommittees, as exemplified by Rockford Public Schools, is one approach to ensuring resolution and communication. It ensures that problems will not solely be resolved at the bargaining table, which allows tension at the school and district level to continuously escalate. Allowing issues to linger also diverts attention from, or progress towards, improving outcomes in teaching and learning and ensuring that all students have access to a high quality education—an outcome that cannot afford to be jeopardized.

# Appendix (Chapter 4)

## Interest-Based Process Resources

**Tool 1: Principles and Interests** Developed by the Massachusetts Education Partnership, this one-page document describes the difference between positions and interests and provides a concrete example that can help to create a common understanding for new ways of thinking about issues. The document can also be used to launch team members into the concept exercises shown in figure 4.1. For a copy of this foundational document, please visit renniecenter.org/IETresources.

**Tool 2: Process Checklist** This tool was designed by the Massachusetts Education Partnership to provide teams with a high-level summary of IBP, as well as to guide them through the process of determining interests and expanding options. Teams are encouraged to use this tool to ensure that IBP principles are being upheld and that IBP processes are being followed. For a copy of the checklist, please visit renniecenter.org/IETresources.

**Tool 3: Shifting the Frame: Example new and old behaviors** Adapted by the Massachusetts Education Partnership for use in districts, this tool was originally designed by Kaiser Permanente's Labor-Management Collaboration. The tool graphically represents the behavior shifts that must occur across stakeholder groups to fully use IBP for negotiations. Conveniently, this tool can be used with stakeholders experienced with IBP, as well as newcomers to the process. For a copy of the graphic, please visit renniecenter.org/IETresources.

*Tool 4: Issue Analysis Worksheet* Developed by Joseph Cutcher-Gershenfeld, the Issue Analysis Worksheet provides a template for teams to use when working through individual issues. Easily adaptable for use at and beyond the bargaining table, the worksheet asks teams to identify the issue, state their interest in its resolution, define other stakeholders' interests, consider power relations, and devise options to consider during issue resolutions. The worksheet is available in Joel Cutcher-Gershenfeld, "Interest-Based Bargaining," in *The Oxford Handbook of Conflict Management in Organizations* (New York: Oxford, 2014), 150. Additionally, it may be found by searching online for both for the author's name and the worksheet's name.

# CHAPTER 5

# *Putting It All Together*

## COLLABORATING ON MEANINGFUL REFORMS

A S YOU MOVE THROUGH THE NEEDS ASSESSMENT, prob-
lem identification, team formation, and initial team process, everything can have the appearance of moving along smoothly and productively.
Unfortunately, these are the easiest parts of LMC collaboration. The biggest challenge begins when the team moves toward evaluating options for
reform efforts to address the identified issues. Any reform that is intended
to improve student outcomes will eventually require behavior change, and
the threat of change is when we see many ostensibly strong collaborations
break down. Of all the steps outlined in the book, this chapter is probably the
most critical—putting it all together to collaborate on meaningful reforms
that improve student outcomes.

Focusing on a specific and collaboratively developed reform helps break
down barriers and galvanize the LMC team. It motivates the team through
difficult times. The challenge is identifying an issue that is meaningful to
all stakeholders and under the control of the team. The LMC team must also
find a way to connect its collaborative work to those who are closest to students—principals, teachers, counselors, social workers, afterschool leaders,
and parents. In this chapter, we identify four criteria that can serve as a guide
for making the final choice and implementing your reform initiative. Many

reform efforts that fit these criteria and address identified root problems are prevalent in public school systems across the United States. To begin this chapter, we summarize these four criteria. To deepen our understanding of the criteria, we examine the implementation of specific reform initiatives. We contrast the examples of peer-assistance-and-review and instructional coaching, highlighting key drivers in decision-making processes. We then consider the case of Revere, Massachusetts, where extended learning time and a new teacher evaluation system were both implemented—each at a time and under conditions that allowed the reform initiative to succeed.

## WHAT IS MEANINGFUL REFORM?

Reform efforts developed and implemented through the LMC process should be more comprehensive and far-reaching than the usual day-to-day work in a school or district. After all, you are involving multiple stakeholders from across the community with the goal of developing a solution to a problem that is better than what each group could have come up with on its own. Consequently, the solutions developed should both be important to all of those involved in the LMC team and directly address student learning. This can be a challenge not only for community stakeholders, who may feel disconnected from what goes on in the classroom, but also for superintendents, union representatives, and district leaders who face pressure to find quick fixes and take a unilateral approach.

Indeed, models of leadership in education far too often expect one individual to do it all. While this perspective may center on the district superintendent or classroom teacher, it is perhaps most exemplified by the expectations we place on school principals. Principals oversee all elements of school operations from budget management and staff development to student discipline and transportation. Of course, it makes sense that we place a strong emphasis on building leadership. There is widespread recognition that effective leaders are the primary drivers of high function schools.[1]

However, our traditional model of school leadership and its focus on the talents and expertise of a single individual are outdated. The complex range of skills and competencies we expect students to master to be successful in the twenty-first century require models of distributed leadership, where decisions are shared across a school or school system.

Taking a more multifaceted approach to leadership where attention to operations management (e.g., budgeting, scheduling, safety, and facilities) is balanced by support for instructional quality and student learning is also supported by research.[2] As Rubinstein and McCarthy showed in their 2014 study of thirty schools in California, stronger partnerships as indicated by the density of professional networks and frequency of adult interactions led to improved student performance.[3] So, we know that sharing leadership across stakeholders and within schools is critical to improving student outcomes. The question that remains is what work, when shared, has the most impact on student learning? To find an answer, we suggest the LMC team assess a jointly developed solution by four criteria:

- Does the reform effort address a root problem identified in the needs assessment and team process?
- Does the reform effort feel important to all stakeholders?
- Does the reform effort connect directly to student learning?
- Is the reform effort within the locus of control of the LMC team and others responsible for implementation?

*Address a root problem.* The reform effort must be tightly linked to the needs assessment explained in chapter 2. Doing so ensures that the effort is based on facts and performance data, and that there is a common perception about what problem is being addressed. The effort must also focus on the root cause of a problem and not its symptoms. Following the strategies outlined in chapter 3 will help the team uncover the root cause driving the problem identified in the needs assessment.

*Important to all stakeholders.* The reform must be compelling and important to all stakeholders on the team. As noted, this may be a challenge, particularly for community stakeholders. District and union leaders on the LMC team may feel compelled to move quickly to find a solution to a problem, such as modifying a teacher evaluation system or strengthening professional development systems. Although these may be compelling reform efforts to all parties, care must be taken to listen to community stakeholders' concerns and integrate their feedback into the design of any solution. Importantly, each member of the team must be able to articulate why the problem and potential solution are compelling.

*Connected to student learning.* This may seem like an obvious criterion—that the reform must be connected to student learning—but our experience with LMC teams led us to state it explicitly. One challenge is that nearly every change in a school or district has the appearance of being linked to student learning. Certainly one could argue that changing bus schedules or meals served impacts student learning. However, what matters most happens in defined learning environments through the interaction of teachers and students with rich content, frequently referred to as the "instructional core."[4] In order for the reform to affect student learning it must impact the ways students and teachers work together with content. If the LMC team cannot show how their reform does that, then they may need to revisit the identified problem or its root causes.

*Within the locus of control.* There is nothing more frustrating for an LMC team than finding out that they do not have the power or resources to implement the identified reform. Issues that require federal or state funding or contract or policy changes are often not good places to start. Ultimately, the goal is for people at the table to be able to drive meaningful reform through a collaborative decision-making process. Many different types of reform work fit the criteria. In the following sections, we discuss a few of these, including peer-assistance-and-review and instructional coaching.

## MEANINGFUL COLLABORATIVE REFORMS

There are number of potential reform efforts an LMC team could implement. Indeed, the difficulty is not coming up with potential solutions, but finding a solution that aligns with the criteria. Let us consider two common approaches to reform today—peer-assistance-and-review (PAR) and instructional coaching. At first glance, either one of these solutions might be well suited for a district seeking to improve student learning by supporting and developing teacher expertise. Indeed, both approaches capitalize on expert teachers to take on leadership roles to help their peers improve their instruction. As we look at each more closely, however, we will see differences emerge in how each might fit the four criteria for the LMC team.

### Two Different Approaches

Peer-assistance-and-review is an "evaluative" approach, in that districts assign individuals other than the school principal the responsibility of evaluating educators. Figures 5.1 and 5.2 provide an overview of PAR and secondary evaluators. Additional resources are provided in the chapter appendix.[5] Experts suggest that this approach requires a substantial degree

**FIGURE 5.1**    Peer-assistance-and-review (PAR)

**What is PAR?**

- Formal process results in a joint labor-management PAR panel determining educator's final evaluation rating.
- Includes a PAR panel and consulting teacher(s).
- Educator receives feedback from consulting teacher.

**Goals of PAR**

- Through the consulting teachers, educators have increased access to high-quality feedback in addition to feedback from their administrators.
- Consulting teacher roles and PAR panel provide leadership opportunities for effective educators.
- Evaluator workload is reduced by distributing evaluation responsibilities.

**FIGURE 5.2**    Secondary evaluators

---

**What are secondary evaluators?**

- Formal process results in multiple evaluators determining educators' final evaluation rating.
- Involves at least two evaluators, often a principal and another educator with content/grade level expertise.
- Educator receives feedback from multiple evaluators.

**Goals of secondary evaluators**

- By having multiple evaluators, often at least one with a similar content or grade-level background, educators have increased access to high-quality feedback.
- Secondary evaluator roles provide leadership opportunities for effective educators.
- Evaluator workload is reduced by distributing evaluation responsibilities.

---

of preparation and training and should be adopted only after carefully considering observation protocols, data collection methods, and feedback processes to prioritize educator growth and development.

In contrast, instructional coaches and collaborative learning are "non-evaluative" approaches. Non-evaluative approaches focus on expanding opportunities for educators to observe peers, jointly review curricula, and co-plan classroom activities. Figures 5.3 and 5.4 provide an overview of instructional coaches and collaborative learning.[6] Instructional coaches are often building leaders (e.g., department heads), trained teacher leaders, or even external consultants, who provide non-evaluative feedback. Collaborative learning may include peer learning through study sessions, informal classroom observations, or instructional rounds. The goal is to increase opportunities to recognize effective practice and encourage open classroom environments without the potential pressure of additional evaluative experiences.

### Matching Reform to the Criteria

Is one approach better than the other? The answer lies in whether one approach might be a better fit for the challenges facing a particular district

**FIGURE 5.3**   Instructional coaches

### What are instructional coaches?

- Coaches are non-evaluative and do not give input into evaluation ratings.
- Coaching role may be full-time or may be in addition to traditional teaching responsibilities.
- Coaches may work with educators who opt in to the support OR with new and/or struggling educators. They may also work with teams of educators.

### Goals of instructional coaches

- Instructional coaches can often provide more frequent and in-depth feedback and coaching to educators compared to evaluators who may have large evaluation caseloads.
- Instructional coaching roles provide leadership opportunities for effective educators.
- Reduces evaluator workload by having instructional coaches observe educators and provide feedback more frequently than required as part of evaluation.

---

**FIGURE 5.4**   Collaborative learning

### What is collaborative learning?

- Collaborative learning structures give educators a chance to observe and provide feedback to one another that is non-evaluative.
- It may include the identification of model teachers or model classrooms, or any teacher may able to open up his/her classroom for observations.
- The focus is on building a culture of collaboration and feedback among educators in a low-risk environment.

### Goals of collaborative learning

- Collaborative learning structures provide an opportunity for peers to give and receive feedback.
- They provide leadership opportunities for all teachers interested in opening their classrooms and/or helping structure the program.
- Builds trust, collegiality, and a culture of shared responsibility for all students, and encourages innovation and risk-taking.

---

given the context and current political climate. Again, the four criteria serve as a guidepost for which might be the best fit for the LMC team to undertake. Let us consider each of the four criteria in turn as they apply to the example of PAR and instructional coaching.

*Does the reform effort address a root problem identified in the needs assessment and team process?* Fully answering this question takes a careful review of the result of the root cause analysis described in chapter 3. A PAR approach brings deeper attention to self-analysis and reflection in order to improve teaching and better meet the needs of a specific group of students. In contrast, an instructional coaching approach is aimed at building teacher knowledge by capitalizing on exceptional teachers who can help train peers on best practices. Each is better suited to a particular type of root cause. For example, if the root cause analysis identifies that teachers have insufficient training in teaching the content set out by the standards, an evaluation process is unlikely to resolve the problem, and therefore coaching and collaborative learning may be more effective for improving student achievement. If, on the other hand, a key issue is that teachers believe they need greater autonomy and professional authority to innovate the curriculum to meet individual student needs, coaching may not produce the desired result. In this case, PAR might help by enabling a self-reflection process that helps teachers understand how changes might impact particular student groups, such as English language learners. By closely tying the reform initiative to the identified need and data, the LMC team can better support those who work directly with students.

*Does the reform effort feel important to all stakeholders?* A key challenge in meeting this criterion is ensuring that all parties can agree on the reform. It is natural for tensions to arise when diverse groups are at the table. For example, coaching may feel important to groups of teachers, whereas community members and district leaders might lean toward the accountability provided by evaluation. To make the reform feel important to all stakeholders, the LMC team needs a clear vision of how the approach will lead to improvement for all parties. Again, one indication that it is important to all stakeholders is that all members of the team can clearly articulate the importance and goals of the reform strategy.

*Is the reform connected directly to student learning?* Improving teaching and learning in a district is almost never an incidental outcome; instead, it requires a "laser focus" on students' needs and the importance of the instructional core. If we go back to our example strategies, we see that part of conceptualizing PAR or instructional coaching as a reform initiative is an ability to clearly explain how the process will directly support student learning. PAR can simply become another bureaucratic process that ultimately takes time away from teaching; coaching can drain resources—including excellent teachers—away from the classroom. Conversely, there are contexts in which either would be an ideal way to further student learning.

We can do a thought experiment to further illustrate the connection to student learning. Districts A and B face a similar challenge of test scores dropping as students enter middle school and move on to high school. After the root cause analysis, District A finds that a key source is a high turnover of teachers who quickly burn out without leadership opportunities. In District B, a major root cause is middle and high school teachers who do not have the training to promote academic reading and writing skills in their content-area instruction. By focusing closely on an evaluation system such as PAR that offers leadership and greater pay opportunities to teachers, District A might be able to better retain talented teachers, thereby directly changing students' experiences in the classroom. In District B, instructional coaches might allow content-area teachers to hone their practice in literacy, an area supplemental to their core expertise, and thus not a focus of evaluation. By closely connecting the approach to the needs of student learners, districts can better meet this criteria; if there is not a direct link to student learning, the reform initiative may not be the best fit.

*Is the reform effort within the locus of control of the LMC team and others responsible for implementation?* There are many elements to being able to implement a reform initiative. Are there sufficient resources in place? Is there adequate cultural readiness and political will to embrace the initiative?

Sometimes a reform initiative may address the root cause, feel important to all the stakeholders in the LMC team, directly connect to student learning, yet not succeed because the timing is not right due to the political climate or even policy and funding changes. For example, there may simply be insufficient funding for instructional coaches due to budget cuts. One key pattern that appears across case studies in this book is that where reform efforts were successful, there was groundwork in place to support them. If the success is beyond the locus of control of the LMC team, it is time to adapt the initiative to take an appropriate first step, or to consider an entirely different approach.

### Getting to Work

To deepen our understanding of how LMC teams can best implement reform initiatives, we look to the case of Revere Public Schools, as described in the following section. Revere has implemented two major reform initiatives to help student achievement—Extended Learning Time (ELT), and a new educator evaluation system. These reforms were both implemented at a specific moment in the history and needs of the district. At the time they were getting off the ground, both fit the four criteria we outline in this chapter. However, the results might have been very different if the district had focused first on evaluation. This case helps us understand how meeting the four criteria sets up the success of the reform initiative.

## COLLABORATING FOR EXTENDED LEARNING TIME IN REVERE

The city of Revere is located just north of Boston along the Atlantic coast. It is a Gateway City, defined by the Massachusetts Legislature as a midsized urban center where the median income and educational attainment of residents fall below state averages. In 2014–15, the Revere school system enrolled approximately 7,000 students. Nearly 60 percent of enrolled students were classified as high-needs, and 55 percent had a first language that was not English.[7] The district's graduation rate was 82 percent.[8]

Despite limited resources and significant social and economic needs, Revere Public Schools (RPS) is widely recognized as a top-performing urban school district in Massachusetts. Step into the Staff Sergeant James J. Hill Elementary School—a Level 1 school in the state's accountability system—and visitors will find innovative classroom environments aligned with best practice.[9] In 2012, for example, the Hill School joined an ongoing statewide extended learning time (ELT) initiative, redesigning and expanding its schedule to add more than three hundred hours for student learning.[10] More importantly, added time and resources were used constructively to forge external partnerships and improve teaching and learning. The Hill School has worked with the Achievement Network to develop systems for assessing student learning and supporting data-driven decision making, and the Bay State Reading Initiative provided school personnel with instructional coaches to make better use of new information and improve classroom practice.

A typical Hill School classroom is now characterized by a dynamic small-group design where students transition between peer-led activities and individualized learning on computers, as well as engage teachers in facilitated small-group discussions. Parent volunteers are readily present, allowing teachers to differentiate learning and focus on individual student needs. Students themselves not only gain proficiency in core academic subjects, but also build competencies in essential social-emotional skills, such as self-management, relationship skills, and responsible decision making.

At the core of the Hill School's success and the gains that have been made districtwide is a productive relationship between labor and management that has been steadily strengthened over the course of the last decade. In considering whether to participate in the ELT initiative, former superintendent Paul Dakin reached out to all eleven district schools for feedback and met with then president of the Revere Teachers Association Susan Lanza.[11] Both Dakin and Lanza were in agreement that ELT would bring new resources to the district and improve academic learning, as well as, in

Lanza's words, "showcase our collaborative leadership style to the community and school stakeholders."[12]

Dakin visited all RPS schools interested in the ELT initiative and held informational meetings with staff. Schools that chose to participate established planning committees made up of central office staff, school administrators, and classroom teachers. At the same time, Dakin worked directly with Lanza on a trust agreement that laid out legal parameters for the program (e.g., work hours, pay scales). Not surprisingly, the union endorsed each ELT plan and the general trust agreement given that teachers had a significant voice in each stage of the decision-making process.[13] ELT initiatives were launched at the Garfield Middle School and A. C. Whelan Elementary School in 2008, followed by the Hill School in 2012. In a national report on ELT initiatives, Dakin stated that "the level of collaboration among all stakeholders led to strong plans that were eventually funded by the state," and both Dakin and Lanza "credited their strong professional relationship as an important contributing factor."[14]

### Emergence of the Revere Educators Leadership Board

RPS's commitment to labor-management collaboration was not in service of a singular program or initiative. Relationships and agreements forged through the adoption of ELT provided confidence to engage in further experimentation. In 2010, RPS chose to be an "early adopter district" in implementing Massachusetts's newly devised educator evaluator system. Educator evaluation has proven to be a major challenge for numerous Massachusetts school districts. In charging toward the front lines, RPS recognized that the design and adoption of new evaluation measures would only be successful if classroom teachers were directly engaged and involved in planning and rollout.

To address this concern, RPS created the role of Evaluation Teacher Leaders. These positions were open to all teachers and, ultimately, at least two individuals were selected for each school. The district reportedly focused on identifying individuals "who were well known and well respected by their peers."[15] Teacher leaders were charged with becoming experts on evaluation processes and providing guidance to district management on how best to introduce changes in district policy and/or school practice. In this role, they become invaluable sources of support not only for their peers, but also for district evaluators responsible for assessing educator effectiveness. The district reported that teacher leaders helped increase acceptance and buy-in, while fear of the new evaluation system decreased. Teacher leaders ultimately played a critical role in shaping understanding of educator evaluation. The term "evaluation" increasingly fell into disuse, as both management and staff saw it less as a punitive measure than a process committed to improving teacher growth and support.

Multiple years of success in designing and implementing potentially contentious reforms (e.g., ELT, educator evaluation) led the district to ask: how can we expand our model of leadership to provide teachers with greater voice and authority in other aspects of district work? The district began to engage in a deliberate planning process to think through and identify areas where collaboration and shared decision making would enhance adult behaviors and improve student learning outcomes. The result was the creation of the Revere Educators Leadership Board, or RELB.[16]

The RELB is comprised of eighty teachers and administrators from across the district, including the union president and superintendent. Representatives are granted release time for meetings that occur during the school day and are compensated for commitments that extend outside contractual time. They come from the district office, the school building, and the classroom at the elementary, middle, and high school levels. The RELB's composition ensures that all stakeholders working on RPS's core education mission have voice and agency, and efforts are also under way to expand RELB participation to include greater community representation (e.g., school committee members, parents, and community-based organizations).

The RELB works closely with central office staff to ensure that various district initiatives are clearly communicated, aligned, and principally focused on improving student learning experiences and outcomes. Perhaps most notably, the RELB has become responsible for overseeing district initiatives or "change processes" to achieve the following goals:

- engage all members of our educational community in the decision-making process
- ensure rigor and relevance throughout all curricular areas
- ensure positive relationships among all members of the school community
- foster resilience within all members of the school community
- foster and celebrate innovation throughout our system[17]

The work of the RELB is undergirded by seven leadership councils. Each council is cochaired by a teacher and an administrator and includes two RELB members. The remainder of the council is comprised of building-level personnel, including principals, school administrators, teachers, aides, and support staff. Councils generally total between ten and twelve members. New council members are frequently recruited to ensure balanced and diverse representation across schools and professional roles. Councils meet for two hours each month, although it is typical for members to address work between meetings. Again, teachers are compensated for their time at their contractual hourly rate for their participation in meetings.

The councils are best thought of as subcommittees to the RELB, effectively coordinating leadership and management responsibilities. Whereas the RELB provides for districtwide strategic planning and goal setting, the leadership councils often execute work necessary to the design, implementation, and evaluation of specific initiatives. The councils' work and accompanying recommendations are presented to the RELB and, sometimes, directly to the Revere School Committee. Councils' particular areas of focus include:

- teacher recruitment, hiring, and placement;
- mentorship and induction;
- professional development;

- educator growth;
- teacher leadership and career ladders;
- organizational structure; and
- adult professional culture.[18]

With this new decision-making structure in place, the district began to once again look critically at increasing teacher leadership opportunities, this time at the school level.

### Distributed School Leadership Through Peer Assistance

In the fall of 2014, RPS engaged in a rigorous planning process to refine its educator evaluation system and place greater emphasis on individual growth and support. Led by the RELB, RPS rebranded its approach to evaluation as an educator growth system and focused on enhancing school-building leadership through a program modeled after peer-assistance-and-review. PAR is premised on the notion that experienced, highly skilled teachers should play a substantial role in supporting and evaluating effective classroom practice. Returning to the idea of teacher leaders, trained reviewers serve as mentors and evaluators for new and veteran teachers alike. Through classroom observations and cycles of critical reflection, reviewers both *assist* teachers in working to improve their practice and provide *reviews* that may become part of their formal evaluation. PAR has been found to improve student achievement and teacher retention, as well as provide an effective method for counseling out of the profession teachers who struggle to improve sufficiently.[19] It has been successfully implemented in a small number of districts across the nation, but it has not been widely implemented, especially in New England.

The goal of RPS's peer assistance program is to build organizational structures that allow teachers "to collaborate, innovate, and take on leadership roles while remaining in the classroom." More specifically, the RELB is focused on improving the quality and accuracy of the feedback that teachers receive through observation of their practice. It is important to note that RPS chose not to include a formal review process in its peer assistance model. Formal evaluations, including classroom observations, are still conducted by an administrator. All administrators were trained through Research for Better Teaching on observing and analyzing teachers prior to assuming their roles as evaluators and are prepared to provide thoughtful feedback on effective pedagogy and classroom practice.[20] Yet challenges remain. Levels of content knowledge across academic disciplines vary among administrators, and classroom teachers may have difficulty providing honest reflection about their practice, shortcomings, and needs when conversations are connected to decisions on job retention and dismissal. While not completely alleviating these concerns, RPS's peer assistance program has shifted attention away from evaluation and placed an explicit emphasis on professional growth by recognizing and promoting teachers' own inherent expertise. Teachers have a direct and specific role in guiding and supporting the conduct of their peers and may eventually help shape evaluation outcomes and staffing determinations—decisions historically made by management.

During the 2016–17 school year, RPS began training approximately thirty consulting teachers to serve as leaders in piloting the peer assistance program. Preliminary approval has been granted by the Revere School Committee for this pilot to launch in 2017–18 with four consulting teachers and forty-eight participating teachers. These consulting teachers will be responsible for observing peers and providing high-quality and timely feedback in addition to that received through formal evaluation processes. In addition, consulting teachers are expected to share information about the peer assistance program to increase teacher interest and improve understanding of the role of evaluation in improving educator growth and support. As current RPS Superintendent Dianne Kelly stated, "We want the program to become a club everyone wants to join." Consulting teachers will work on the leading edge of a districtwide effort to shift cultural norms to where conversation and collaboration between colleagues is a standard of leadership. These are big aims. But the RELB believes sustaining RPS's success depends on all educators assuming responsibility for school improvement.

This outcome will only be achieved if all educators believe they are empowered to lead in this effort.

## CONCLUSION

This chapter makes the argument that to achieve sustainable education reform, we must reconsider how "things get done." In an era when cultural norms and technological requirements are constantly in flux, and definitions of success can abruptly change, progress is best achieved by leaders who recognize and confront the delicate interplay between *thinking* and *doing*, empowering others to act in the pursuit of shared goals. School change is only possible when adults in schools—teachers and leaders alike—take responsibility for changing their practice to ensure that all students learn at high levels.

Throughout this book, we pay careful attention to the collaborative process of identifying a problem that all groups can get behind. What we emphasize here is that the final selection of a problem of practice requires all of the careful attention and reflection at every step of the process. After all, there are no easy solutions for problems related to student learning and achievement gaps. By undertaking a self-assessment to determine if the selected reform initiative fits the four criteria described above, we can move forward with implementation knowing that the hard work ahead is built on a solid foundation.

# Appendix (Chapter 5)

## Reforms Resources

*Tool 1: An Interactive Planning Guide for Distributed Leadership*
Developed by the Massachusetts Department of Elementary and
Secondary Education, the Planning Guide is for districts interested
in using distributed leadership approaches to help improve the
quality of feedback and instruction in their schools. Teams comprised of district- and school-level administrators, union leaders,
and classroom teachers are encouraged to use this tool to determine
readiness for distributed leadership and to develop strategies for
implementation. The Planning Guide is open source and available
at www.doe.mass.edu/edeval/leadership/.

*Tool 2: A User's Guide to Peer Assistance and Review* Developed by
researchers at the Harvard Graduate School of Education, the
User's Guide provides case examples, resources, and research on
planning, implementing, and sustaining PAR program in your district. Resources can be found at http://www.gse.harvard.edu/~ngt/
par/resources/.

*Tool 3: Boston Public Schools' PAR Program* One of the goals of Boston's
PAR program is to serve as a model to other districts that might
also be interested in building a similar program. The website provides free resources and examples at https://bostonpar.wordpress.
com/resources/.

***Tool 4: Literacy Coaching Clearinghouse*** This site offers an array of policy and practice briefs and coaching tools for literacy coaches, teachers, administrators, and researchers. For specific tools, such as a protocol for observations or conducting team meetings, see http://www.literacycoachingonline.org/tools.html.

**CHAPTER 6**

# When Things Go Wrong

## GETTING BACK ON TRACK AND SUSTAINING COLLABORATION

I N PREVIOUS CHAPTERS, we examined specific tools for advancing labor-management-community collaboration to help drive district and school improvement. A potential consequence of this approach is to present collaboration as a linear or orderly process with specific starting and end points, resulting in quickly realized changes in educational practice. If only it were this easy! Collaboration cannot be forced. It is an arduous process that requires participants to confront deeply embedded differences in their values and goals for education. This challenge is compounded by the fact that collaboration rarely goes as planned; leaders come and go, local elections produce unexpected results, and external shocks, such as budget cuts, introduce new tensions. Such disruptions can undermine, or lead to the suspension of, collaborative activities. All of which leads to a crucial question: what should district and school leaders do when things go wrong?

Answering this question requires rethinking how we approach education reform. Tony Bryk and others have argued that districts and schools struggle to improve when they "implement fast" but "learn slow," moving rapidly from one reform strategy to the next, often in response to a perceived lack of progress.[1] Such approaches strain resources, incite conflict, and erode trust. Leaders and practitioners become overwhelmed by the relentless layering of divergent ideas and proposed solutions. Instead, districts, schools, and communities must "learn fast to implement well." Reform strategies should evolve, but as the result of continuous assessment of programming against specified indicators of progress, rather than knee-jerk reactions to perceived successes or failures.

In this chapter, we acknowledge that something always goes wrong. Mistakes are to be expected and, in fact, should be viewed as necessary to the improvement process. Without learning from what has been previously tried, progress cannot be made. Successful collaborations thrive by developing trust and creating systems and structures to sustain that trusting relationship. Trust emerges over time through the processes outlined in the first five chapters of this Guide. Trust ensures that the collaboration extends beyond personal relationships. By following the steps described here, LMC teams should also move toward creating standing collaborative structures—committees, teams, or governing boards—to monitor and assess decisions, utilize data and research to make adjustments to policies and programming, and communicate changes to the larger community. Taken together, the trust and structures that emerge enable collaborators to build a coherent change management system designed to support ongoing work toward achieving long-term goals, but prepared to engage in successful corrections of immediate and short-term difficulties.

From this perspective, robust collaborations are closely aligned with the principles of implementation science, popularized in the field of education by Bryk and others, and defined as the scientific study of methods for implementing research into policy and practice. Through the lens of implementation science, leaders and educators are engaged in repeated cycles of inquiry aimed at the continuous improvement of programming and practice. Understanding stages of implementation helps LMC teams adjust to unexpected events. LMC teams should view implementation as a continuous process that involves multiple steps, and should remember that collaboration is dynamic and evolves as implementation progresses.

Keeping the big picture in mind, the LMC team is not undone by the outcomes of particular strategies, but views each new piece of information, both positive and negative, as an opportunity to strengthen its overall reform effort. In the following section, we discuss more fully the basic tenets of implementation science to help ground discussion. We then look more explicitly at the application of implementation science to the field of education, sharing and summarizing an approach developed by Bryk and colleagues. In the latter half of the chapter we present a case study on Leominster Public Schools, a higher performing urban school district in Massachusetts that has successfully overcome various struggles in its collaborative efforts at reform by working to develop a more coherent and structured approach to change management. We conclude the chapter by analyzing lessons learned from Leominster's experience.

## IMPLEMENTATION SCIENCE: THE BASICS

Implementation science is defined as the study of the systemic introduction and integration of research methods and findings into routine practice to improve the quality and effectiveness of program outcomes.[2] One way to think of implementation science in more concrete terms is that practitioners engage in repeated cycles of inquiry to evaluate immediate and short-term changes in practice and enable corrective action before programming is fully implemented, heightening the likelihood of success.

For example, an LMC team may wish to provide enhanced and jointly implemented professional development to better align teaching with new learning standards. Rather than providing training and then waiting until the end of the school year to see if student achievement improves on standard assessments, the collaborative team would come together to jointly plan for how best to support improvements in teachers' instructional methods. Critically, they would identify driving factors that can accelerate or undermine instructional delivery, as well as a range of quantifiable immediate, short-term, and long-term outcomes they expect to achieve. The implementation of professional development opportunities would then be married to a robust research program to collect data and analyze progress in achieving specified goals. Corrective action may then be taken based on research findings produced while implementation is still ongoing. This process, known as a "plan, do, study, act cycle" (PDSA), is expected to repeat itself throughout the life of the program, allowing for the continuous refinement and improvement of reform strategies.[3]

Implementation science offers a carefully structured process based on the tenets of PDSA. The first five chapters of this Guide covered the planning step in detail. When LMC teams emerge from the planning stage, they should have defined the dimensions of the intended practices they hope to change, identified the root causes that influence the practice, and established a culture of collaboration. That said, a key point of implementation science is that teams do not assume to know all potential factors at the beginning of implementation. Additional factors will be identified as implementation proceeds.

Indeed, implementation science identifies four stages to implementation, and the planning phase is just the beginning. These stages—exploration (planning), installation, initial implementation, full implementation—also occur in a continuous process, similar to the plan, do, study, act cycle.[4] As noted in the previous chapter, it is when solutions emerge and start being tested—at the installation stage—that collaborations often breakdown. LMC teams should keep in mind that installation is just the very beginning of the process. This can be hard to do, particularly if the team spent a considerable amount of time working together to plan the reform. Acknowledging that the months spent together conducting a needs assessment, identifying root causes, and refining team processes was only one step in a full implementation cycle can be hard. But understanding that LMC collaboration and implementing reform is an ongoing process helps put challenges in perspective. Seemingly unsolvable problems or conflicts are only a part of the ongoing four-stage implementation process.

It is important to note that like most collaborative activities these stages are neither linear nor separate. Stages of implementation happen dynamically according to the organizational context, human resources, and implementation history of each practitioner community. Figure 6.1 illustrates each stage of implementation.

1. *Exploration.* The readiness of the community to engage in an improvement process is assessed. The needs assessment (chapter 2) is conducted at this stage and a team is formed (chapter 3). The team begins a process (chapter 4) and starts putting together an initial plan, including the examination of key intervention components and identification of implementation drivers that will facilitate changes in practice (chapter 5).

2. *Installation.* Initial steps of resource gathering, allocation, and alignment with community needs begin to take place. The LMC team and other stakeholders responsible for implementation need to support the organization and staff in preparing to move forward. This

**FIGURE 6.1**    Plan, Do, Study, Act graphic

**Implentation Stages**

2–4 Years ⟶

| Exploration | Installation | Initial Implementation | Full Implementation |
|---|---|---|---|
| • Assess needs<br>• Examine intervention components<br>• Consider implementation drivers<br>• Assess fit | • Acquire resources<br>• Prepare organization<br>• Prepare implementation drivers<br>• Prepare staff | • Adjust implementation drivers<br>• Manage change<br>• Deploy data systems<br>• Initiate improvement cycles | • Monitor, manage implementation drivers<br>• Achieve fidelity and outcome benchmarks<br>• Further improve fidelity and outcome |

*Source:* http://socialwork.oxfordre.com/view/10.1093/acrefore/9780199975839.001.0001/
acrefore-9780199975839-e-949

process may include developing learning communities to facilitate learning and strengthen community buy-in for pursuing large-scale change.

3. *Initial implementation.* The first pieces of feedback on implementation are gathered and processed. A support system is needed to assist the LMC team in initiating work, managing change processes, deploying data systems, and realigning implementation drivers to stay consistent with project goals. These support systems should be found at the school, district, and community levels.[5]

4. *Full implementation.* In the final stage of implementation, the LMC team has established a culture of improvement, where mistakes and unexpected problems are treated as learning opportunities, not derailments. Leaders have proven able to survive loss of expertise through staff departures. Managers and administrators are able to continuously adjust organizational support to adequately assist and facilitate the improvement work of the educators and practitioners. Further, there is strong evidence of implementation fidelity based on routine assessments of progress toward specified and refined indicators.

In the next section, we look at the particular case of Leominster Public Schools, where progress has been tempered by setbacks and threats to the survival of reform efforts. The story of Leominster documents how collaborative practice can be leveraged to develop sustainable improvement, but without a focused effort to transition to a more rigorous and structured process aligned with the tenets of implementation science, gains are hard to sustain.[6]

## LEOMINSTER AND THE DISTRICT CAPACITY PROJECT

Leominster joined the District Capacity Project (DCP) in 2012, the year it was inaugurated. The District Capacity Project enables LMC teams to identify common educational interests and implement evidence-based strategies to advance student learning. Operating as part of the Massachusetts Education Partnership (MEP), the DCP entails a significant commitment by Massachusetts education leaders representing both management and labor to work together to support education innovation. The MEP Governing Board includes leadership from the 22,000-member American Federation of Teachers–Massachusetts, the 750-member Massachusetts Association of School Superintendents, the 2,400-member Massachusetts Association of School Committees, and the 110,000-member Massachusetts Teachers Association, along with representatives from four of the Commonwealth's most prominent education research institutions: Massachusetts Institute of Technology, Northeastern University, the University of Massachusetts Boston, and the Rennie Center for Education Research & Policy, which serves as the MEP's managing partner. The Massachusetts Department of Elementary and Secondary Education is a nonvoting member of the board.

Local teams participating in the DCP consist of superintendents, union representatives, school committee members, administrators and teachers, and community leaders. The teams utilize collaboration and interest-based processes (IBP) to productively address education reforms mandated by the state or initiated internally at the district or school levels. Consistent with effective collaborative practice, work operates at two levels. First, teams develop skills and capacities to enact concrete and timely plans aimed at addressing pressing educative needs. Second, teams serve as launching points for deeply embedding collaborative practices throughout district and school decision-making and implementation processes to guide future reform efforts. The DCP's overarching goal is to instill a culture of improvement that prioritizes student growth and learning; promotes educator leadership and ownership of practice, including participation in governance; embraces continuous improvement, allowing for both successes and setbacks; and seeks engagement among all community members.

### Building Resilient Collaboration in Leominster

Located in north central Massachusetts, Leominster Public Schools serves nearly 6,000 students across three preK early learning centers, four elementary schools, two middle schools, and three high school programs. The diversity of school options and alternative pathways at the secondary school level is notable. The district supports a traditional comprehensive high school with an enrollment of approximately 1,800 students, but also oversees a vocational technical school and a small alternative school, the Leominster Center for Excellence (LCE), which emphasizes student advisories, personalized learning plans, flexible scheduling, and real-world learning opportunities through internships in local businesses, nonprofit organizations, and community service.[7] The district's portfolio of education programs from preK into postsecondary is designed to serve a diverse and at-risk population. Roughly half of the students enrolled in Leominster Public Schools are considered high-needs due to economic disadvantage, demographic risk factors, learning disability, or English language learner status.

Despite these challenges, Leominster has achieved considerable success. For the past five years the district's four-year graduation rate has been about 90 percent, with only one school failing to meet accountability targets. Leominster's interest in and decision to participate in the District Capacity Project emerged not from a perception of crisis or need, but rather from a strong desire to build on current success by improving educator supports within the school system. In fact, Leominster already had a collaborative culture based on a preexisting foundation of successful labor-management meetings during prior collective bargaining sessions. Local leaders had also previously participated in notable capacity-building initiatives such as the state's New Superintendent's Induction Program and the District Governance Support project, sponsored respectively by the Massachusetts Association of School Superintendents and Massachusetts Association of School Committees. Such pre-work meant that both labor and management leaders were well prepared to pursue collaboration.

After Leominster formally joined the DCP at the beginning of the 2012–2013 school year, it formed a collaborative team composed of the superintendent, the Leominster Education Association (LEA) president, school committee representatives, and other management and labor representatives.[8] Year one was marked by rapid initial success, exceeding the rate of change and scale of impact in other communities involved in the DCP. In particular, Leominster succeeded in creating a formal teacher leadership program. During the 2012 winter, the team decided to focus on rewarding teacher performance with the hope of incentivizing exemplary teachers to engage in and eventually lead professional development, mentoring, innovative curriculum development, and the creation of special projects. The thought process was that competitively compensating teachers, through a new and innovative teacher compensation model, would lead to improvements in student achievement. The team identified and researched different teacher compensation models. However, upon reflection, members found they were not comfortable with any of the models they reviewed. In addition, union leaders dismissed out of hand any models based on merit pay or student test score performance. This entire process was guided by an assigned third-party facilitator who was a former labor leader with vast experience as a facilitator in collaborative practice. While disagreements emerged, enthusiasm among the team remained strong. The team's commitment to its overall purpose of identifying and supporting teachers as leaders within the district remained intact.

In January 2013 the team shifted its focus to look at career ladders and teacher leadership programs, and began to focus on creating a new Teacher Leader program, which created additional work time and compensation for those highly effective teachers that desired to engage in curriculum development, mentoring, and peer development work. In the spring of 2013, a memorandum of understanding was drafted between the district and union, and the proposed program was formally adopted by both the union and school committee. This successful collaboration between labor and management leaders created seven Teacher Leader positions.

Three elements should be highlighted in examining Leominster's initial success. First, as noted above, Leominster already had significant experience with collaborative practice. The district has had previously used interest-based processes to successfully negotiate its last contract. Second, the move to establish the Teacher Leader program corresponded closely to Leominster Superintendent Jim Jolicoeur's strategic vision for the district. Hired in July 2011, Jolicoeur had extensive experience in the private sector as well as over a decade of experience as an assistant superintendent in two nearby districts. His vision included tapping teachers who were thriving in the classroom to help drive further innovation and entrepreneurship through enhanced instructional practice, resulting in expanded academic achievement and success. Third, Leominster took on a project that required contract negotiations relatively early in the work. Thus, all the work of the team was codified in a memorandum of understanding, which eventually could be integrated into future contract negotiations. This approach offered short-term stability in collaborative decisions. However, it would later on prove to undermine trust as proposed alterations were often viewed as a perceived attempt to reopen negotiations.

### Bumps in the Road

In the second year of work, challenges began to emerge. The team endeavored to move beyond a specific program objective (e.g., Teacher Leaders) and pushed for creating new district and school decision-making processes based on interest-based practices. The team proposed to expose all staff to interest-based processes through a professional development day or staff meeting, followed by school-based trainings on IBP facilitation. The first, and perhaps most enduring, challenge to emerge was difficulty in translating year-one gains into an embedded culture of improvement. Year-two goals seemed disconnected from the team's original focus on promoting teachers' professional growth, resulting in a series of disjointed and problematic improvement strategies.

Early in year two, for example, the team and facilitator decided to tackle the difficult topic of teacher compensation, setting their sights on an ambitious plan to transform the salary schedule from fourteen steps to three. Not only did this new strategy have little to do with the Teacher Leader program or the team's newly stated purpose of using IBP practices to guide school-level decisions, but it also introduced a politically contentious issue that highlighted the limitations of Leominster's collaborative work. Issues in communication began to divide members. The union president and labor representatives on the team remained strongly committed to the collaborative process and were open to discussing teacher compensation, but it became apparent that the union's executive board was not well informed about the work. Compounding deficiencies in information flow was the fact that changing the teacher salary scale was a contractual issue that required ratification by the union. A general lack of awareness and broad-based support among labor made it difficult to reach timely agreements. Trust began to falter.

Leadership changes also introduced new tensions, especially in the absence of a coherent communication structure, further reducing project stability. Specifically, at the start of year two, a new union president was elected. The newly elected president pushed the collaborative team to focus on developing deeper, more significant engagements with teachers beyond the teacher leadership positions. These efforts led to changes in team membership designed to ensure that classroom teachers were well represented across disciplines, grades, and experience levels. While these steps further empowered and involved teachers in the collaborative processes, they also further reduced participation among the union's executive board. It became less and less clear whether the team's work was representative of a shared vision between union and administrative leaders, or a select group of teacher leaders. The team itself was no longer well positioned to anticipate, confront, and resolve disputes.

Challenges resulting from poor communication, changes in leadership, and loss of trust gradually made the work a space of ad-hoc negotiations and resolution of contentious issues, rather than a steady collaborative process building toward shared, stable, continually assessed improvement strategies. Like many other communities, the team confronted real limitations in terms of the capacity to get things done.

Unfortunately, year three in Leominster was marked by a significant decrease in collaborative activities. Only four team meetings were held in the 2014–2015 school year. Circumstances external to the team's work, most notably some key staffing changes in school leadership, continued to erode trust among the superintendent and several members of the union's executive board. Further, the entire system was affected by the fact that the district's labor contract was about to expire. Concerns about budgetary expenditures and the perceived unfairness of cost-of-living adjustments for educators' salaries (comparatively lower than other city employees) were a point of disagreement. (This is a key reason why the team attempted to address teacher salary scales in year two.) The union's executive committee pointed out that significant funds were being expended on personnel with no direct link to support of student learning, and that qualified educators were choosing to leave the district due to working conditions.

Yet, despite the internal challenges and external pressures that negatively impacted the collaborative work through its second and third years, two clear constants remained. First, the efficacy of the labor-management collaboration proved adept at yielding positive results when focused on specific programmatic activities, exemplified by the Teacher Leader program. Second, the team persevered through periods of internal dissension and difficult contractual negotiations to remain committed to collaborative work. This commitment was demonstrated in the fourth year when Leominster plunged forward, while still struggling to set a clear agenda for its work. Superintendent Jolicoeur's belief in a culture of collaboration and distributed leadership was a key element in regaining momentum.

The team entered its fourth year with new members and a renewed purpose to regain lost ground and rebuild damaged trust between management and labor. A number of major shifts occurred. The union election saw another new president elected. In addition, there were several new school committee members, and a new third-party facilitator. The team began by reexamining the Teacher Leader program and asking themselves if it was well designed to support their principal goal of providing for professional growth among all teachers. After a period of reflection, the team reached agreement to transfer a portion of the Teacher Leader funding toward the development of a professional resource network (PRN) model in its early childhood, elementary, and middle schools. The goal of the peer resource network is to assist all teachers in meeting the demands of the Massachusetts new curriculum frameworks (which are aligned with the Common Core State Standards). This redeployment of funding and the development of the PRN expanded schools' capacities to support the development of enhanced instructional practices in the classroom.

The team diligently communicated decision making and new programming to the larger school community, providing time to receive and incorporate feedback. A renewed collaborative spirit enabled the team to work with district and school leaders to address sticky problems, like adjusting school calendars to allow for common planning time. As the fourth year began to close, the team moved forward with a pilot proposal to support four resource teachers in each of the district's two middle schools, three in each of its four elementary schools, as well as two in its early childhood program. The twenty-two resource teacher positions would be offered a stipend of $1,500 for a total budgetary commitment of $33,000. Through a sustained commitment to collaboration and a lived learning experience demonstrating that mistakes happen, difficulties emerge, and work must be reconsidered and adjusted to succeed, the Leominster team appeared to be back on track.

In the next section, we reflect on lessons learned from the Leominster case study and how the district's experience may inform efforts to grow systemic improvement plans in education settings over time.

### Lessons Learned: Implementation as a Process

The Leominster case study, when considered in parallel to the precepts of implementation science, provides a strong resource for reflection on how to achieve sustainable improvements in LMC collaboration. As noted above, the literature on implementation science outlines four principal stages in improvement programs attempting to reach sustainability and capacity to scale. In the Leominster case, looking in detail at the core components of these stages reveals areas of limited attention that perhaps account for the district's growing pains in establishing resilient collaboration. In the exploration stage, Leominster assembled a highly qualified team, expending much time and effort toward choosing individuals with expertise in collaborative practice or IBP, and providing significant training to those who had less experience. On the other hand, diversity was a challenge. It was not until year two that representatives from across the teaching profession were included. Furthermore, the only community stakeholders involved were school committee members.

In the initial implementation stage, it is clear that most stakeholders, and in particular the district and the third-party facilitator, continuously worked to achieve buy-in for the collaborative process. However, the absence of internal team support structures and external system-level supports to assist in the implementation process were revealed to be major shortcomings. Finally, the full implementation stage was never completely reached at Leominster. While a large audience was engaged in collaborative decision making, the original design of the Teacher Leader program had a limited impact on the full workforce. Struggles with communication and program expansion meant the leader program, while viewed as successful, was never implemented as fully intended. Recent corrective measures to create a more widespread professional resource network are seeking to remedy this problem, but they are just now getting underway.

The Rennie Center has developed a framework to extend LMC collaboration in order to sustain teams through the four stages of implementation.

This framework is divided into two distinct parts: the "What" and the "How."[9] Table 6.1 provides a basic overview of the "What."

LMC team members begin by asking themselves what is the purpose of their improvement strategy. This includes identifying, measuring, and monitoring the quantifiable and verifiable outcomes they hope to achieve. By quantifiable, we mean setting accountability benchmarks that hold all stakeholders and practitioners, as well as participating institutions, accountable for improvement. By verifiable, we mean assessing the implementation progress against these accountability benchmarks. This step helps ensure that improvement actions remain results-oriented by linking both short-term and long-term assessments of progress to measurable changes

**TABLE 6.1**   The What

| Core elements | Component |
|---|---|
| Identify a problem of practice, define key drivers for improvement, build a logic model for improvement | • Build a common understanding of a shared problem of practice<br>• Determine an interrelated set of hypotheses about key drivers for practice improvement<br>• Examine systems that produce problem of practice |
| Detail the nature of the intervention toward well-defined beneficiaries, and ground the intervention in best practices | • Programmatic components rooted in best practices and expert opinions<br>• Strategies to achieve and coordinate improvement practices<br>• Understanding the characteristics that a group of practitioners have in common, and the school's socio-political-cultural context in which the implementation program will operate |
| Establish quantifiable and verifiable projected outcomes | • Define the quantifiable objectives we commit to achieve<br>• Clear definition / choice of progress and accountability benchmarks<br>• Verification mechanisms |

*Source:* Rennie Center for Education Research & Policy, *Change Management Framework* (Cambridge, MA: Rennie Center, 2016).

in practice. Of course, designing an effective system for collecting and analyzing data on outcome measures can be difficult, and may exceed local expertise and resources.

A useful strategy is the creation of research-practice partnerships with nearby universities or other research organizations, providing implementing teams with access to experts in the field. For example, the Massachusetts Institute for College and Career Readiness matches tenured university faculty with urban school districts to assist in the design, implementation, and evaluation of comprehensive college and career pathways. With each district's blessing, these researchers take the lead on assessing processes and program outcomes throughout the duration of the project. The researchers benefit from access to local actors and data, which can be difficult to collect, and from opportunities to engage in more applied work.

Regardless, it is critical that any system for tracking outcomes adhere to rigorous research standards in the interest of eliminating test bias and ensuring proper representation of complex systems. This includes setting clear guidelines for collecting, storing, tracking, and using data. Strong data collection and analysis systems enable improvement programs to not only assess progress, but also to effectively manage their own capacity, examine variations from expected outcomes, differentiate among variations resulting from predictive behaviors within the improvement process and problems with the overall plan, and then reorient programming as needed.

Once team members have fully detailed what they hope to accomplish, they must ask how they will achieve their improvement aims and effectively execute underlying strategies. Table 6.2 presents the next phase of the Rennie Center's framework: the "How."

As explored throughout this chapter, the "how" means stakeholders must work as committed and trusting teams. A common understanding of a problem and its root causes is only valuable if members agree that acting to solve it is a shared priority.[10] As we described in chapter 2, committed and trusting teams emerge by creating safe spaces for interactions to take place, which includes agreeing on shared values and norms, creating

**TABLE 6.2** The How

| Core elements | Component |
|---|---|
| Committed and trusting team | • Commitment to a problem as a shared priority |
| | • An agreement on roles and responsibilities |
| | • Diversity of stakeholders |
| | • Norms of behavior and accountability |
| | • Safe space: learning is the paragon |
| Effective operations | • Adequate resources for improvement support, research validation, and scaling |
| | • Effective communications plan: new expertise processed in the same way, to build a shared language and knowledge base with scaling intent |
| | • Clear action plan with transparent tasking processes, made robust by regular check-in protocols |
| Systemic testing and learning | • Improvement is results-oriented, continuous, fidelity- and reliability-oriented |
| | • Improvement activity has multiple iterative cycles of test-and-measurement process |
| | • Improvement ensures systemic learning and scaling capacity |

*Source:* Rennie Center for Education Research & Policy, *Change Management Framework* (Cambridge, MA: Rennie Center, 2016).

familiarity through consistent engagement, and willingly assessing the costs and benefits of proposed actions to all stakeholders. Trust also depends on a team's capacity for empathy, respect, flexibility, listening, and interest in others' ideas. While we often think of such characteristics as innate, they are skills to be developed through the processes laid out in this Guide. Teams may engage in trainings and workshops on building trust as they launch improvement plans to better understand and further develop the team's capacity to work with one another. An added incentive is that high-trust teams tend to be more innovative and open to considering a broader range of interests and options.

Once trust is established teams must learn how to function effectively as discussed in chapter 3. Ensuring success in the teaming process is aided by establishing clear and agreed upon expectations and norms of behavior. Teams benefit from drafting a statement that declares their commitment to improvement, as well as clearly defining team roles and responsibilities (e.g., governance, membership, schedules, staffing, communication, and conflict resolution) through formal protocols.

To sustain collaboration, LMC teams must also establish an effective system of operations to manage change and support data-driven decision making.[11] Teams must have adequate resources for improvement support and research validation, including human and managerial resources to support data analysis, research, operational management, and resource allocation. Effective operations also include constructive communication. Communication is important for any innovation, as it is not always clear how new knowledge or practices will be processed and understood. Teams must think through how best to disseminate information and establish a shared knowledge base to support scaling. Intentionally linking communication protocols to decision-making processes and the implementation of new practices may help establish a transparent feedback process toward participating practitioners and the community, creating a more hospitable learning environment. Further, taking time to develop a common language or shared terms of reference may be a critical element of community building and improvement sustainability.

Effective operations benefit from a results-oriented action plan, which may also be called a process map, run chart, or solution system, and is used to visualize specific actions that may be taken to achieve improvement goals. The action plan takes its cues from the implementing team's working theory of action as exemplified in documents like a driver diagram, but it is far more focused on the identification and management of daily tasks and routines. An action plan may be used to assign roles and responsibilities, track a project timeline and deadlines to be met, allocate resources, and chart milestones or growth targets expected to be achieved at specific

**FIGURE 6.2**  Plan, Do, Study, Act cycle

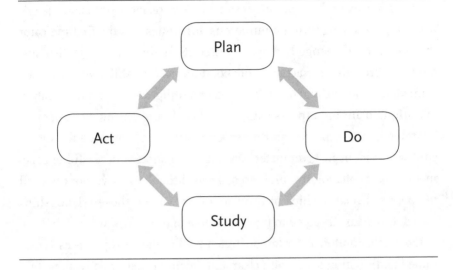

stages. Action plans are necessary to maintain fidelity to the community of practice's commitments, as described in the shared project statement.

Finally, collaborative teams must engage in systemic testing. Improvement occurs when teams are results-oriented and focus on the continuous review of reliable data and information. They engage in disciplined inquiry focused on sustainability of the improvement system, fidelity of implementation, and adherence to prescribed practice. Ultimately, developing a plan to test improvement strategies (Plan), carry out the test (Do), observe and learn from results (Study), and finally determine what modifications should be made (Act), drives an approach to reform focused on continuous improvement, rather than on success or failure in achieving set goals (see figure 6.2).

## Conclusion

One of the strongest indicators of how deeply collaborative practice has been embedded is the ability of leaders and practitioners to continue to find ways to work together when things go wrong. Implementation of education reform tends to be a "stop and start" process. The unexpected occurs, reforms evolve, and progress stalls. The resiliency of Leominster's team in persevering through numerous difficulties was the first indicator that a culture of change had been created. Nonetheless, to establish sustained improvement practices, collaborators need to shift away from the immediacy of action and fast-paced implementing, and toward the creation of a strong planning process with defined goals and outcomes, supported by implementer expertise and managerial structure. The need for such a shift was evident in Leominster. Despite the district's successful engagement in past collaborative processes, it was difficult to move work beyond the personal relationships of team members. When those relationships frayed, the team struggled to figure out how to move forward.

Once collaborators have demonstrated a willingness to operate as a committed and trusting team, with clear agreement on roles and responsibilities, it is important to incorporate other indicators or drivers of success into improvement plans. Collaborators must have access to adequate resources and established protocols for engaging in essential planning activities, such as operational management, data analysis, and research. Resources and expertise can be augmented through external partnerships.

In addition, sustainable improvement plans benefit from establishing a coherent management structure, which may be conceptualized as an effective operations center, and a clear plan of action for monitoring processes, assigning tasks, and ensuring a robust check-in protocol. Effective operational management helps keep work in line with implementation science precepts, prioritizing the building of capacity to rapidly analyze continuous feedback. Data is gathered and analyzed in a transparent and consistent manner, helping build a language and knowledge base that can be shared with all project participants. Changes in practice are therefore not seen as a retreat from shared goals, undermining trust and collaboration, but as a logical response to new information.

Finally, improvement processes must embrace the scientific and data-driven approach of implementation science. For best practice, any initiative should work through multiple test-and-measurement cycles. Collaborative histories in places like Leominster provide a strong foundation for driving improvements in teaching and learning. Realizing the potential of LMC collaboration means building a commitment to pursuing an implementation plan that is results-oriented, as well as communicating purposely around desired outcomes and progress. These are the data-driven requirements that underwrite the capacity of an improvement effort to ensure systemic learning and scaling capacity.

# Conclusion

On the first pages of this book, we offered collaboration as a strategy for reform in addressing some of the most vexing educational problems our education system is facing today, including moving the needle on academic achievement for our most vulnerable student populations. Throughout the book we have provided a number of case studies where districts were able to create meaningful and effective reform by bringing together the diverse interests of the district, labor union, and community members.

As much as we believe in the power of collaboration, we understand why most reform initiatives are still implemented by a small number of district leaders. Schools today face unprecedented pressures: standards-based accountability in an age of ever-shifting standards; rapid demographic shifts including increasing numbers of students who are learning English as they learn academic content; a funding climate that can limit resources. These are just a few of the problems that confront districts and make it difficult to have the time or energy to reach out to others. We also acknowledge that including a diverse group of stakeholders in the planning and implementation of educational reforms can slow the change process down. Collaboration can be a frustrating experience, especially for superintendents and senior district leaders who face daily pressures to show demonstrable improvement in student learning (e.g., test scores). Faced with the choice to reach out to others, who may not always have a productive or research-based theory of improvement, many educational leaders choose otherwise. Alternatively, they may incorporate diverse stakeholders into the decision-making process, but only in superficial ways that often do more harm than good.

Despite all these challenges, we argue that it is not only more effective to collaborate, but that collaboration is a mandatory component for effective and lasting educational reform. In a country founded on immigration, such as the United States, the challenges of educating an incredibly diverse student population are amplified. Overcoming the effects of poverty, limited opportunities, and inequality require that people and the organizations they lead work together. For example, there will be little progress on readying children for kindergarten unless an entire ecosystem of organizations and service providers work together. Every touchpoint in the child's life—pre-natal, birth, early child care, nutrition, and so on—needs people working together to ensure that the child eats nutritiously, has a safe and enriching home environment, and feels cared for and loved. That means doctors, parents, caregivers, librarians, community providers, healthcare and social service workers, and early childhood teachers must all work together. And for that to happen, the district, union, business, and community leaders must commit to creating and sustaining systems and structures that facilitate collaboration.

What we provide you here is a process that ensures that your commitment of time and resources will pay off over time. As we saw in Baltimore, it was Superintendent Alonso's careful investing in the community that resulted in the bond needed to finance the reform he designed with the teacher union. In Revere, it was the thoughtful implementation of extended learning time that allowed the district to move forward into the often murky waters of teacher evaluation. And in Rockford, educational leaders' commitment to the interest-based process ensured that difficult conversations could take place, not derail progress, and keep everyone moving forward together. Over and again, collaboration resulted in forward momentum. Most importantly, that momentum was shown in example after example to benefit students.

In this Guide, we have provided a step-by-step process for communities to build the type of collaboration that leads to collective impact—long-term commitments by diverse stakeholders to a common agenda for improving student learning and reducing inequality. The first step is to understand what collaboration is, and what it isn't. Our definition of collaboration serves as a foundation on which to build an engaging and inclusive *process through which stakeholders who see parts of a problem differently can explore these differences and construct solutions that are better than what they could have come up with on their own.*[1] With the end goal identified, the next step is to identify the starting point with a comprehensive needs assessment. The assessment brings to light differing views of stakeholders concerning the major issues and helps build buy-in and motivation for change. Forming a team and then having members work together productively is the next step. As we saw in Fall River, five core strategies—establishing a compelling team purpose, composing the team thoughtfully and intentionally, creating space and time to team, generating team norms, and clearly defining roles and responsibilities—are critical to effective collaborative teamwork.

Perhaps more importantly, teams should use an interest-based process to support productive, not destructive, conflict. Using IBP means considering many possible solutions and then focusing on those that are both realistic and address all stakeholders' interests. In chapter 5, we argue that any identified problem should fit four criteria. The problem should 1) address a root problem identified in the needs assessment, 2) feel important to all stakeholders, 3) connect directly to student learning, and 4) be within the locus of control of the team. Of course, things will eventually go wrong, even if all goes smoothly at first. When conflict seems insurmountable or leadership turnover threatens sustainability, it is important to remember that these and other challenges are all part of an implementation process. Stepping back and understanding the big picture of exploration, installation, initial implementation, and full implementation will bring perspective and help identify necessary steps to get things back on track.

As we close this book, we want to take a moment to focus on our true North Star, and that is our students. They are the reason we sit down through tense meetings and force ourselves to remain open to critical feedback. We find again and again that when LMC teams are at an impasse, putting the students first—explicitly focusing on their needs—can get the ball moving again. Indeed, research on group dynamics shows that having a shared goal brings diverse parties together and allows them to find solutions. Creating a better future for our students is the universal value that brings us all together.

Indeed, this is an exceptional time in the moral arc of our country. Never in recent times has our country been more polarized, and never has the opportunity to set a unifying and revitalizing vision been greater. What can we do to work together more effectively for the betterment of our communities? What can we do to bring children, families, and adults from different backgrounds—rural, urban, black, white, wealthy, and poor—together to solve problems, build a stronger future, and love one another?

We offer a solution that is practical and hands-on, and that can make a difference in any community in the United States. It is a solution that is easy to talk about, but hard to do well. In a time of rapid change, we ask that you slow down and commit to a long-term process. This involves deliberately bringing diverse parties to the table, spending time deeply understanding the needs of the district and their root causes, then carefully selecting reform that best meets the causes and not the symptoms. Successful collaboration also means weathering the storms of implementation, because problems will undoubtedly arise as a reform initiative moves from the planning stages to the realities of rollout.

Collaboration is incredibly difficult, but its potential to solve deeply entrenched social problems is limitless. If we are truly serious about ensuring that our children have the skills, experiences, and character to build a brighter future, then there is only one choice. We must all work together.

# Notes

## INTRODUCTION

1. Barbara Gray, *Collaborating: Finding Common Ground for Multiparty Problems* (San Francisco: Jossey-Bass, 1989), 1–25.
2. Andrew H. Van de Ven, "On the Nature, Formation, and Maintenance of Relations Among Organizations," *Academy of Management Review* (October 1976): 24–36; Peter S. Ring and Andrew H. Van de Ven, "Structuring Cooperative Relationships Between Organizations," *Strategic Management Journal* 13, no. 7 (1992): 483–98; Ranjay Gulati, *Managing Network Resources: Alliances, Affiliations, and Other Relational Assets* (New York: Oxford, 2007).
3. Lisa B. Bingham and Rosemary O'Leary, "Conclusion: Parallel Play, Not Collaboration: Missing Questions, Missing Connections," *Public Administration Review* 66 (2006): Suppl. S; Chris Huxham and Siv Vangen, *Managing to Collaborate : The Theory and Practice of Collaborative Advantage* (New York: Routledge, 2005); Elizabeth Lank, *Collaboration Advantage* (New York: Palgrave Macmillan, 2006); Michael Winer and Karen Ray, *Collaboration Handbook: Creating, Sustaining, and Enjoying the Journey* (Saint Paul, MN: Amherst H. Wilder Foundation, 1994).
4. Morten T. Hansen, *Collaboration: How Leaders Avoid the Traps, Create Unity, and Reap Big Results* (Cambridge, MA: Harvard Business Press, 2009).
5. National Commission on Teaching and America's Future, *Reducing the Achievement Gap Through District-Union Collaboration: The Tale of Two Districts* (NEA Foundation, 2007); Linda Kaboolian and Paul Sutherland, *Win-Win Labor Management Collaboration in Education* (Cambridge, MA: Rennie Center for Education Research & Policy, 2005).
6. Adam Urbanski, "Improving Student Achievement Through Labor-Management Collaboration in Urban School Districts," *Educational Policy* 17, no. 4 (2003): 503–518.

7. Susan Moore Johnson and Morgan L. Donaldson, "The Effects of Collective Bargaining on Teacher Quality," in J. Hannaway and A. J. Rotherham, eds., *Collective Bargaining in Education: Negotiating Change in Today's Schools* (Cambridge, MA: Harvard Education Press, 2006).

8. Dan Goldhaber, "Are Teachers Unions Good for Students?" in Hannaway and Rotherham, eds., *Collective Bargaining in Education:* 141–158.

9. National Commission on Teaching and America's Future, *Reducing the Achievement Gap.*

10. Kaboolian and Sutherland, *Win-Win Labor Management Collaboration.*

11. Jonathan Eckert, *Local Labor-Management Relationships as a Vehicle to Advance Reform: Findings from the U.S. Department of Education's Labor-Management Conference* (Washington, DC: US Department of Education, 2011).

12. Geoff Marietta, *The Unions in Montgomery County Public Schools,* S. M. Johnson, ed. (Cambridge, MA: Harvard Education Press, 2011).

13. John McCarthy and Saul A. Rubinstein, *Reforming Public School Systems Through Sustained Union-Management Collaboration* (Washington, DC: Center for American Progress, 2011); Saul A. Rubinstein and John McCarthy, *Union-Management Partnerships, Teacher Collaboration, and Student Performance* (New Brunswick, NJ: Rutgers, 2014).

14. Greg Anrig, *Beyond the Education Wars: Evidence That Collaboration Builds Effective Schools* (Century Foundation Press, 2013); New Jersey Department of Education, *New Jersey Statewide Assessment Reports,* 2012, www.state.nj.us/education/schools/achievement/index.html.

15. Ken Futernick, Sara McClellan, and Scott Vince, *Forward, Together: Better Schools Through Labor-Management Collaboration* (San Francisco: WestEd, 2012).

16. Allyne Beach and Linda Kaboolian, *Working Better Together: A Practical Guide to Help Unions, Elected Officials and Managers Improve Public Services* (Washington, DC: Working For America Institute, 2013).

17. US Department of Education, *Shared Responsibility: A US Department of Education White Paper on Labor-Management Collaboration,* 2012, http://www2.ed.gov/documents/labor-management-collaboration/white-paper-labor-management-collaboration.pdf ; "A New Compact for Student Success: The Principles of Student-Centered Labor-Management Relationships" (presentation for Advancing Student Achievement Through Labor-Management Collaboration Conference, Denver, CO: February 15–16, 2011), http://www.ed.gov/labor-management-collaboration/conference/compact.

18. Barry Bluestone and Thomas Kochan, *Toward a New Grand Bargain: Collaborative Approaches to Labor-Management Reform in Massachusetts* (Boston: Boston Foundation, 2011), http://50.87.169.168/Documents/EPRN/Collaborative-Approaches-to-Labor-Management-Reform-in-Massachusetts.pdf.

19. For example, Robert Axelrod in *The Evolution of Cooperation* (New York: Basic Books, 1984) set up computer tournaments of the Prisoner's Dilemma game

theory to closely mimic human interactions. In thousands of games using dozens of different strategies, the consistent winner always cooperated first and then imitated their opponent's moves. The best outcome occurred when both opponents cooperated with each other on each move.

20. Eric L. Trist, "Referent Organizations and the Development of Interorganizational Domains," *Human Relations* 36, 1983: 269–284.

21. John Kania and Mark Kramer, "Collective Impact," *Stanford Social Innovation Review* (Winter 2011): 35–41.

22. Terry M. Moe, "Union Power and the Education of Children," in Hannaway and Rotherham, eds., *Collective Bargaining in Education*: 229–255; Terry M. Moe, *Special Interest: Teachers Unions and America's Public Schools* (Washington, DC: Brookings Institution Press, 2011).

23. Steven Brill, *Class Warfare: Inside the Fight to Fix America's Schools* (New York: Simon and Schuster, 2012).

24. Chris Huxham and Siv Vangen, "What Makes Practitioners Tick? Understanding Collaboration Practice and Practicing Collaboration Understanding," in J. Genefke and F. McDonald, eds., *Effective Collaboration: Managing Obstacles to Success* (New York: Palgrave, 2001), 1–16; Henri Tajfel, *Human Groups and Social Categories* (New York: Cambridge, 1981).

25. Experts in the field use the broader concept of interest-based process. Interest-based bargaining is constrained to negotiations, whereas the interest-based process can be used in a variety of settings. We intentionally use the term interest-based process because the approach can (and should) be used beyond just the bargaining table.

26. Amy C. Edmondson, "The Three Pillars of a Teaming Culture," *Harvard Business Review* (December 2013).

## CHAPTER 1

1. Barbara Gray, *Collaborating: Finding Common Ground for Multiparty Problems* (San Francisco: Jossey-Bass, 1989), 1–25.

2. Allen Grossman and Geoff Marietta, *Montgomery County Business Roundtable for Education* (Cambridge, MA: Harvard Business School Press, 2009).

3. John Kania and Mark Kramer, "Collective Impact," *Stanford Social Innovation Review*, Winter (2011): 35–41.

4. For this section we draw on two case studies written about the collaborative work in Baltimore by faculty and staff with Harvard University's Public Education Leadership Project (PELP). Harvard Graduate School of Education Professor Susan Moore Johnson, Harvard Business School Professor John J-H Kim, and PELP research assistants Geoff Marietta, S. Elisabeth Faller, and James Noonan wrote a case study on the teachers' contract work in Baltimore, *Career Pathways, Performance Pay, and Peer-review Promotion in Baltimore City Public*

*Schools* (Cambridge, MA: Harvard University Public Education Leadership Project, 2013). Harvard Graduate School of Education Professor Karen Mapp and James Noonan wrote a case study on family and community engagement, *Organizing for Family and Community Engagement in the Baltimore City Public Schools* (Cambridge, MA: Harvard University Public Education Leadership Project, 2015).

5. Johnson, Kim, Marietta, Faller, and Noonan, *Career Pathways.*
6. Ibid.
7. Mapp and Noonan, *Organizing for Family and Community Engagement.*
8. Ibid.
9. Ibid.
10. Ibid.

## CHAPTER 2

1. John Kotter, *Leading Change* (Cambridge, MA: Harvard Business Press, 2012).
2. Rennie Center for Education Research & Policy, *Labor-Management-Community Collaboration in Springfield Public Schools* (Cambridge, MA: Rennie Center, 2012).
3. Robert Forrant, "Winners and Losers: High-Tech Employment Deals an Uneven Hand," *Massachusetts Benchmarks* 4, no. 3 (2001): 12–16; Robert Forrant, "Too Many Bends in The River: The Post–World War II Decline of the Connecticut River Valley Machine Tool Industry," *Journal of Industrial History* 5, no. 2 (2002): 71–91; City of Springfield Planning Commission, *Presentation at the Urban Land Institute September 24–29, 2006,* http://www.springfieldcityhall.com/planning/fileadmin/Planning_files/Springfieldpanel.pdf; D. Ring, "House Oks Bailout Bill; Board Would Get Sweeping Powers," *The Republican,* June 24, 2004.
4. Ring, "House Oks Bailout Bill."
5. P. Goonan, "New Budget Still Raises Concerns," *The Republican,* June 22, 2003.
6. The percentage of students from low-income backgrounds had increased by nearly 17 percentage points between 1994 and 2004; by 2004 77 percent of students in Springfield were low-income. See Massachusetts Department of Elementary and Secondary Education, *State and District Profiles: Springfield Public Schools,* http://profiles.doe.mass.edu.
7. In 2004, only about half of students graduated from high school in four years, the percentage of students proficient in English language arts remained in the mid-30s for all tested grades (i.e., 36, 35, and 32 percent in grades 4, 7, and 10, respectively), and only a quarter of fourth graders and fewer than one in ten eighth graders were proficient in math. See Massachusetts Department of Elementary and Secondary Education, *State and District Profiles: Springfield Public Schools,* http://profiles.doe.mass.edu.
8. Rennie Center, *Labor-Management-Community Collaboration.*

9.  Andrew Churchill and Sharon Rallis, *Using KEYS 2.0 District-wide: A Springfield, Massachusetts Case Study* (Amherst, MA: University of Massachusetts Center for Education Policy, 2009): 11.

10. Ibid., 18.

11. Ibid.

12. Ibid., 25.

13. Massachusetts Department of Elementary and Secondary Education, *State and District Profiles: Springfield Public Schools*, http://profiles.doe.mass.edu/.

14. During contract negotiations in the spring of 2006, the FCB wanted to include a value-added measure of student achievement as a component in the teacher evaluation. After a series of impasses, SEA took the issue to arbitration. In the fall of 2006, a state arbitrator ruled that the proposed value-added measure could not be used in the teacher evaluation. SEA and the FCB then bargained for the Springfield Teacher Evaluation and Development System (STEDS).

15. PBIS is a prevention-based behavior management system that incorporates data and evidence into a team-based decision-making process. See Bob Algozzine et al., *Evaluation Blueprint for School-Wide Positive Behavior Support* (Eugene, OR: National Technical Assistance Center on Positive Behavior Interventions and Support, 2010), www.pbis.org.

16. Consortium for Educational Change, "About," http://cecillinois.org/about.

## CHAPTER 3

1.  Anthony S. Bryk, Louis M. Gomez, Alicia Grunow, and Paul G. LeMahieu, *Learning to Improve: How America's Schools Can Get Better at Getting Better* (Cambridge, MA: Harvard Education Press, 2015), 61; Susan Albers Mohrman, Susan G. Cohen, and Allan M. Morhman Jr., *Designing Team-based Organizations: New Forms for Knowledge Work* (San Francisco: Jossey-Bass, 1995), 10.

2.  Rennie Center for Education Research & Policy, *Staying the Course: Sustaining Improvement in Urban Schools* (Cambridge, MA: Rennie Center for Education Research & Policy, and Edvestors), http://www.edvestors.org/wp-content/uploads/2016/05/Staying-the-Course-Full-Report-Web-Version.pdf.

3.  Saul A. Rubinstein and John E. McCarthy, "Teachers Unions and Management Partnerships: How Working Together Improves Student Achievement," *Center for American Progress* (2014).

4.  Bryk et al., *Learning to Improve*, 61; Mohrman et al., *Designing Team-based Organizations*; Amy Edmondson, Richard Bohmer, and Gary Pisano, "Speeding Up Team Learning," *Harvard Business Review* 79, no. 9 (2001): 125–134.

5.  Barbara Gray, *Collaborating: Finding Common Ground for Multiparty Problems* (San Francisco: Jossey-Bass, 1989).

6.  Charles Duhigg, "What Google Learned from Its Quest to Build the Perfect Team," *New York Times Magazine* (2016).

7. Anita Williams Woolley, Christopher F. Chabris, Alex Pentland, Nada Hashmi, and Thomas W. Malone, "Evidence for a Collective Intelligence Factor in the Performance of Human Groups," *Science* 330, no. 6004 (2010): 686–688; Alex Pentland, "The New Science of Building Great Teams," *Harvard Business Review* 90, no. 4 (2012): 60–69.

8. Duhigg, "What Google Learned."

9. Vesa Peltokorpi and Mervi Hasu, "How Participative Safety Matters More in Team Innovation as Team Size Increases," *Journal of Business and Psychology* 29, no. 1 (2014): 39.

10. Amhy Edmondson, "Psychological Safety and Learning Behavior in Work Teams," *Administrative Science Quarterly* 44, no. 2 (1999): 360–361.

11. Michael A. West and Neil R. Anderson, "Innovation in Top Management Teams," *Journal of Applied Psychology* 81, no. 6 (1996): 690.

12. Amy C. Edmondson, *Managing the Risk of Learning: Psychological Safety in Work Teams* (Cambridge, MA: Division of Research, Harvard Business School, 2002) 255–276.

13. The "Five Whys" were developed originally as part of the Toyota Production System, and have been adopted and refined as part of the Six Sigma quality improvement process. A similar approach to root cause analysis exists in the Baldridge system and other continuous improvement processes.

14. District Capacity Project, *Understanding the Challenge* (Cambridge, MA: Rennie Center for Education Research & Policy, 2015).

15. Mohrman, Cohen, and Morhman Jr., *Designing Team-based Organizations*, 27.

16. Michael Barber, Andy Moffit, and Paul Kihn, *Deliverology 101: A Field Guide for Educational Leaders* (Thousand Oaks, CA: Corwin Press, 2010), 39.

17. Ibid.

18. John Eric Adair, *Leadership for Innovation: How to Organize Team Creativity and Harvest Ideas* (London, Philadelphia: Kogan Page, 2007), 15.

19. UMass Donahue Institute, "District Capacity Project Evaluation: Findings from the First Two Years of Program Implementation," December 5, 2014, http://www.doe.mass.edu/research/reports/2014/12DCP-EvalReport.pdf, 10.

20. Susan Moore Johnson, Geoff Marietta, Monica C. Higgins, Karen L. Mapp, and Allen Grossman, *Achieving Coherence in District Improvement: Managing the Relationship Between the Central Office and Schools* (Cambridge, MA: Harvard Education Press, 2015), 64.

21. Barber, Moffit, and Kihn, *Deliverology 101*, 41.

22. UMass Donahue Institute, "District Capacity Project Evaluation."

23. MEP District Capacity Project, *Team Ground Rules* (Cambridge, MA: Rennie Center for Education Research & Policy, 2015).

24. Springfield Public Schools, *DCP Work Plan Supplement* (Cambridge, MA: Rennie Center for Education Research & Policy, 2014).

25. David A. Garvin and Michael A. Roberto, "What You Don't Know About Making Decisions," *Harvard Business Review* 79, no. 8 (2001): 110.

26. Ibid., 110.

27. Steven ten Have, Wouter ten Have, Frans Stevens, and Marcel van der Elst, *Key Management Models: The Management Tools and Practices That Will Improve Your Business* (London: Pearson Education, 2003), 20.

28. Gerard H. Gaynor, "Building an Innovation Team," *IEEE Engineering Management Review* 43, no. 2 (2015): 9.

29. All case study research on Fall River Public Schools was gathered by the UMass Donohue Institute, an independent evaluator of the District Capacity Project (DCP).

30. United States Census Bureau, "Quick Facts: Fall River City, Massachusetts," http://www.census.gov/quickfacts/table/PST045215/2523000.

31. Massachusetts Department of Elementary and Secondary Education, "2015 Massachusetts District Report Card Overview: FALL RIVER PUBLIC SCHOOL DISTRICT (00950000)," http://profiles.doe.mass.edu/reportcard/ DistrictReportCardOverview.aspx?linkid=106&orgcode=00950000&fycode=201 5&orgtypecode=5.

32. UMass Donahue Institute, *District Capacity Project Case Narratives: Implementation and Impacts in Four Cohort 1 Districts* (Cambridge, MA: Rennie Center for Education Research & Policy, 2015), 11.

33. Gray, *Collaborating*, 1–25.

34. Amy C. Edmondson, "Teamwork on the Fly," *Harvard Business Review* 90, no. 4 (2012): 78.

35. Constructive conflict is also known as cognitive conflict. Destructive conflict is also known as affective conflict. See Garvin and Roberto, "What You Don't Know," 26.

36. The framework for these section titles was adopted from Edmondson, "Teamwork on the Fly," 78. The section write-ups are strongly related to interest-based processes frameworks.

37. Garvin and Roberto, "What You Don't Know," 29.

38. Mark D. Cannon and Amy C. Edmondson, "Failing to Learn and Learning to Fail (Intelligently): How Great Organizations Put Failure to Work to Innovate and Improve," *Long Range Planning* 38, no. 3 (2005): 315.

39. Adair, *Leadership for Innovation*, 88–89.

40. Ibid., 90.

41. Garvin and Roberto, "What You Don't Know," 29–30.

42. Massachusetts Education Partnership, *Supplement 10: Basic Consensus* (Cambridge, MA: Rennie Center for Education Research & Policy, 2013).

## CHAPTER 4

1. Roger Fisher, William L. Ury, and Bruce Patton, *Getting to Yes: Negotiating Agreement Without Giving In*, rev. ed. (New York: Penguin, 2011).

2. Richard E. Walton and Robert B. McKersie, *A Behavioral Theory of Labor Negotiations: An Analysis of a Social Interaction System* (Ithaca, NY: Cornell University Press, 1965), xx.

3. Joel Cutcher-Gershenfeld, Thomas Kochan, and John Calhoun Wells, "In Whose Interest? A First Look at National Survey Data on Interest-Based Bargaining in Labor Relations," *Industrial Relations: A Journal of Economy and Society* 40, no. 1 (2001): 7–18; Joel Cutcher-Gershenfeld, "Interest-Based Bargaining," in William K. Roche, Paul Teague, and Alexander J. S. Colvin, eds., *The Oxford Handbook of Conflict Management in Organizations* (New York: Oxford, 2014), 3; Scott Hargrove, "Interest-Based Bargaining: Achieving Improved Relationships Through Collaboration," *Library Management* 31, no. 4/5 (2010): 8; Sally Klingel, *Interest-Based Bargaining in Education* (Washington, DC: National Education Association, 2003), 10–11, http://digitalcommons.ilr.cornell.edu/reports/16/.

4. It is important to note that this approach goes by a variety of names in the bargaining field, including: integrative bargaining, win-win bargaining, principled negotiations, getting to yes, problem-solving negotiations, collaborative bargaining, and consensus bargaining. Regardless of what the approach is called, the overall theory, process, and structure for engaging in negotiations is consistent. See Scott Hargrove, "Interest-Based Bargaining: Achieving Improved Relationships Through Collaboration," *Library Management* 31, no. 4/5 (2010): 229–240.

5. Linda Kaboolian and Paul Sutherland, *Win-Win Labor Management Collaboration in Education* (Cambridge, MA: Rennie Center for Education Research & Policy, 2005).

6. Traditional bargaining also has a number of different names, including positional bargaining and concessionary bargaining.

7. Barry Bluestone and Thomas A. Kochan, "Toward a New Grand Bargain: Collaborative Approaches to Labor-Management Reform in Massachusetts," *Members-only Library* (2014): 35.

8. M. Gaffney, *After the Training: A Refresher on Interest-Based Bargaining* (Georgetown, ME: 2013), 16.

9. Fisher, Ury, and Patton, *Getting to Yes.*

10. Joel E. Cutcher-Gershenfeld, "Bargaining Over How to Bargain in Labor-Management Negotiations," *Negotiation Journal* 10, no. 4 (1994): 323–335; Nancy E. Peace, "A New Way to Negotiate—Collaborative Bargaining in Teacher Contract Negotiations: The Experience in Five Massachusetts School Districts," *Journal of Law and Education* 23 (1994): 376.

11. Johanna Macneil and Mark Bray, "Third-party Facilitators in Interest-Based Negotiation: An Australian Case Study," *Journal of Industrial Relations* 55, no. 5 (2013): 705–706.

12. This statement is based on data from the Massachusetts Education Partnership suggesting that from 2012 to 2016, out of 42 bargaining units using IBB for negotiations, 40 chose to use an external facilitator.

13. Peace, "A New Way to Negotiate," 368.

14. Cutcher, Gershenfeld, "Bargaining Over How to Bargain," 326.

15. Fisher, Ury, and Patton, *Getting to Yes.*

16. Answers to figure 4.1: Q1. Position Q2. Perception, Q3. Perception Q4. Interest Q5. Position Q6. Interest Q7. Perception.

17. Pauline Graham, *Mary Parker Follett—Prophet of Management: A Celebration of Writings from the 1920s* (Washington, DC: Beard Books, 2003).

18. Cutcher-Gershenfeld, "Interest-Based Bargaining," 1–2.

19. An independent agency of the US government that specializes in promoting positive labor-management relations across many different sectors.

20. Jerome Barrett, "The Interest-Based Bargaining Story at the Federal Mediation and Conciliation Service," *Negotiation Journal* 31, no. 4 (2015): 432.

21. The approaches lumped under the term IBB here include the US Department of Labor's program of Mutual Gain Bargaining, and the further modifications to the Mutual Gain Bargaining developed by the FMCS in its experience with the P.A.S.T. model (Principles, Assumptions, Steps and Techniques); see Klingel, *Interest-Based Bargaining in Education*, 29.

22. Barrett, "The Interest-Based Bargaining Story," 432.

23. Joel Cutcher-Gershenfeld and Thomas Kochan, "Taking Stock: Collective Bargaining at the Turn of the Century," *Industrial and Labor Relations Review* 58, no. 1 (2004): 3–26.

24. Thomas A. Kochan, Barry Bluestone, and Nancy E. Peace, *Massachusetts Education Partnership: Results and Research from the First Two Years* (Cambridge, MA: Rennie Center Education Research & Policy, 2015), 7–8.

25. Klingel, *Interest-Based Bargaining in Education*, 19.

26. Gaffney, *After the Training*, 6.

27. Ibid.

28. Ibid.

29. Ibid., 9.

30. Ibid., 8.

31. Ibid., 14.

32. Cutcher-Gershenfeld, "Bargaining Over How to Bargain," 331.

33. Fisher, Ury, and Patton, *Getting to Yes.*

34. Adapted from Nancy R. Tague, *The Quality Toolbox*, 2nd ed. (Milwaukee, WI: ASQ Quality Press, 2004), 126–132; Massachusetts Education Partnership, *Supplement #5: All About Brainstorming* (Boston, MA: 2013).

35. Gaffney, *After the Training*, 5.

## CHAPTER 5

1. K. Leithwood, K. S. Louis, S. Anderson, and K. Wahlstrom, *How Leadership Influences Student Learning* (New York: Wallace Foundation, 2004); Michael Onorato, "Transformational Leadership Style in the Educational Sector: An Empirical Study of Corporate Managers and Educational Leaders," *Academy of Educational Leadership Journal* 17, no. 1 (2013).

2. Rennie Center, *The Complex Role of an Effective Principal* (Cambridge, MA: Rennie Center for Education Research & Policy, 2013), http://www.renniecenter. org/research/ComplexRoleEffectivePrincipal.pdf.

3. John McCarthy and Saul A. Rubinstein, *Reforming Public School Systems Through Sustained Union-Management Collaboration* (Washington, DC: Center for American Progress, 2011); Saul A. Rubinstein and John McCarthy, *Union-Management Partnerships, Teacher Collaboration, and Student Performance* (New Brunswick, NJ: Rutgers, 2014).

4. David K. Cohen and Deborah Loewenberg Ball, *Instruction, Capacity, and Improvement* (Philadelphia: Consortium for Policy Research in Education, 1999).

5. Massachuetts Department of Elementary and Secondary Education, *Interactive Planning Guide for Distributed Leadership* (MDESE, 2016), www.doe.mass.edu/ edeval/leadership.

6. Ibid.

7. The Massachusetts Department of Elementary and Secondary Education defines high-needs students as belonging to any of the following subgroups: free and reduced lunch eligible, students with disabilities, English language learners, and former English language learners.

8. Massachusetts Department of Elementary and Secondary Education, *School and District Profiles* (MDESE, 2016), http://profiles.doe.mass.edu/.

9. The Massachusetts Department of Elementary and Secondary Education classifies all districts and schools with sufficient data into one of five accountability and assistance levels. Highest performing districts and schools are classified as level one and lowest performing districts and schools as level five. Determinations are based on the state's Progress and Performance Index (PPI), which combines information about narrowing proficiency gaps, growth, and graduation and dropout rates into a single number from 0 to 100. For more information see http://profiles.doe.mass.edu/state_report/accountability.aspx.

10. The Staff Sergeant James J. Hill Elementary School was previously known as the William McKinley

11. Elementary School. In 2015 the McKinley was renamed as it moved to a new location and building in Revere.

12. Revere Public Schools first joined the statewide extended learning initiative in 2008. Two schools—A. C. Whelan Elementary School and Garfield Middle School—were part of the initial cohort. The Hill School joined the initiative in 2012.

13. Scott Vince, *Materials Overview: Extended Time for Student Learning and Teacher Collaboration* (San Francisco: WestEd), https://www.wested.org/wp-content/uploads/extended-complete-tab.pdf.

14. Ibid.

15. Ibid.

16. Massachusetts Department of Elementary and Secondary Education, *Revere Case Study*, http://www.doe.mass.edu/edeval/leadership/RevereCaseStudy.docx.

17. Another critical factor in developing and maintaining Revere's strong labor-management relationship has been continuity of leadership. Paul Dakin served as RPS's superintendent for fifteen years before retiring in 2015. He was succeeded by Dianne Kelly, an assistant superintendent in the district for five years before her appointment. Seth Daniel, "Dakin Officially Leaves Schools Today," *Revere Journal*, December 24, 2015, http://www.reverejournal.com/2015/12/24/dakin-officially-leaves-revere-schools-today/#.

18. Revere Public Schools, *Mission and Vision* (Revere Public Schools website), http://www.revereps.mec.edu/?page_id=1583.

19. Revere Public Schools, *Brochure* (Revere Public Schools website), http://www.revereps.mec.edu/wordpress/wp-content/uploads/2015/04/Brochure-Revere-Schools-Final.pdf.

20. Susan Moore Johnson and John Papay, *Redesigning Teacher Pay: A System for the Next Generation of Educators* [EPI Series on Alternative Teacher Compensation Systems, no. 2] (Washington, DC: Economic Policy Institute, 2009).

21. Research for Better Teaching, http://www.rbteach.com/.

## CHAPTER 6

1. Anthony S. Bryk, Louis M. Gomez, Alicia Grunow, and Paul G. LeMahieu, *Learning to Improve: How America's Schools Can Get Better at Getting Better* (Cambridge, MA: Harvard Education Press, 2015), 61.

2. Martin Eccles and Brian Mittman, "Welcome to Implementation Science," *Implementation Science* 1, no. 1 (2006).

3. Alicia Grunow, *Improvement Discipline in Pratice* (Carnegie Foundation for the Advancement of Teaching, 2015), https://www.carnegiefoundation.org/blog/improvement-discipline-in-practice/.

4. D. L. Fixsen, S. F. Naoom, K. A. Blase, R. M. Friedman, and F. Wallace, *Implementation Research: A Synthesis of the Literature*, FMHI Publication No. 231

(Tampa, FL: University of South Florida, Louis de la Parte Florida Mental Health Institute, National Implementation Research Network, 2005).

5.  D. K. Aladjem and K. M. Borman, eds. *Examining Comprehensive School Reform* (Washington, DC: Urban Institute Press, 2006).

6.  In the DCP's third year of work, the MEP contracted with the Donahue Institute at UMass Amherst to conduct an independent evaluation of its four oldest collaborative engagements with school districts (Donahue Institute, 2015). Researcher Jen Gordon led the evaluation, which was based on interviews, focus groups, document reviews, and observed practice. One of the studied school districts was Leominster Public Schools (LPS). Much of the following case study is based on Ms. Gordon and the Donahue Institute's work, although information has been updated to be current as of June 2016.

7.  Both Leominster's vocational-technical program and LCE are innovation schools made permissible in Massachusetts through the 2010 Act Relative to the Achievement Gap and defined as in-district schools granted autonomy from traditional governance structures (e.g., scheduling, staffing, budgeting, curriculum).

8.  In the 2014–2015 school year, the DCP added seven new members: three management representatives (including an administrator in human resources; an administrator in curriculum, instruction, and assessment; and a middle school principal) along with four labor representatives, represented by teachers from a diverse range of schools and the LEA's field representative from the Massachusetts Teachers Association.

9.  The terms "what" and "how" used to organize the Rennie Center's framework are drawn from the work of the Billions Institute. For more information see: http://www.billionsinstitute.com/.

10. Amy Edmondson, *Teaming: How Organizations Learn, Innovate, and Compete in the Knowledge Economy* (San Francisco: Jossey-Bass, 2014).

11. While many organizations emphasize the importance of developing a strong center of operations to support and manage collaborative work, the concepts shared in this chapter were specifically informed by the work of the Billions Institute and its focus on large scale change. For more information see: http://www.billionsinstitute.com/.

## CONCLUSION

1.  Barbara Gray, *Collaborating: Finding Common Ground for Multiparty Problems* (San Francisco: Jossey-Bass, 1989), 1–25.

# Acknowledgments

This book would not have been possible without the engagement, openness, and commitment of the districts, unions, and communities working together every day to improve student outcomes. Without their lead in this important work, we would have no examples to draw from or point to for how collaboration can work in any community. Specifically, we would like to thank the labor, district, and community leaders highlighted throughout our book: Baltimore City Schools, Fall River Public Schools, La Grange District 105, Leominster Public Schools, Montgomery County Public Schools, Revere Public Schools, Rockford County Public Schools, and Springfield Public Schools.

It goes without saying that this Guide would not exist without the leadership of the Rennie Center for Education Research & Policy. The exceptional foresight of its founder, former Massachusetts Secretary of Education Paul Reville, to make a long-term commitment to collaboration cannot be understated. Because of that investment, the Rennie Center produced the Labor-Management-Community Collaboration Toolkit, which directly led to the creation of this book. Importantly, the Rennie Center was not on its own. Collaboration experts such as Andrew Bundy, Emily Bozentka, Tim Fitzgerald, Mary Ellen Shea, Nancy Peace, Ron Suga, and Tom Kochan developed many of the tools featured in this book. They, along with District

Capacity Project Facilitators, have been the true leaders in helping communities work together.

The authors would also like to personally thank Harvard Education Press and our wonderful editor, Nancy Walser. Her patience, prodding, and feedback were always appreciated, and made the difference for us. Emily Murphy Kaur would like to thank her husband, Harmeet Singh, for his support during the writing process. Chad d'Entremont would like to thank Damian Boutillon for his help, and his wife, Anna d'Entremont, and family for putting up with him when he was buried in his computer, typing away. Finally, Geoff Marietta would like to thank his mentor Susan Moore Johnson, who showed him the way to productive collaboration in education, and his wife, Sky, for her support and commitment.

# About the Authors

**Geoff Marietta** is an educator, researcher, and entrepreneur who is passionate about helping people work together to improve the lives of children. He serves as the executive director of Pine Mountain Settlement School, a National Historical Landmark serving communities in the coalfields of eastern Kentucky. Marietta is also a research fellow at Berea College, and cofounder of Mountain Tech Media, a diversified media and technology company based in eastern Kentucky. He has written extensively on labor-management-community collaboration in education and is the author of dozens of cases, policy reports, and articles on the topic. After graduating from the University of Montana, Geoff was a teacher and administrator on Navajo Nation in New Mexico. He went on to earn his MBA from Harvard Business School and a doctorate from the Harvard Graduate School of Education, founding a software technology company along the way. Geoff currently lives at Pine Mountain Settlement School in Harlan County, Kentucky, with his wife, Sky, and their sons, Harlan and Perry.

**Chad d'Entremont** is the executive director of the Rennie Center for Education Research & Policy. He is responsible for shepherding the organization's mission to improve public education through deep knowledge and evidence of effective policy making and practice. In this capacity he has coauthored numerous articles, book chapters, and reports on reform strategies ranging from early childhood education to early college designs, and he has launched multiple initiatives to support local communities in the implementation and evaluation of evidence-based practice. In 2012 Dr. d'Entremont help found the Massachusetts Education Partnership, a unique coalition of labor and management leaders committed to working collaboratively to advance sustainable school improvements, and in 2014 he helped found the Massachusetts Institute for College and Career Readiness (MICCR) in partnership with Boston University, the Massachusetts Department of Elementary and Secondary Education, and MassINC, with the support of a $1 million cooperative agreement with the US Department of Education's Institute for Education Sciences. Dr. d'Entremont began his career as a teacher, serving high-needs students in both urban and rural settings. He is the former assistant director of a nationally renowned research center at Teachers College, Columbia University, and from 2007 to 2011 was the research and policy director at Strategies for Children, as well as project manager for Massachusetts's successful application for a $50 million Race to the Top–Early Learning Challenge award. He has a PhD in education policy and social analysis and an MA in the sociology of education from Teachers College, Columbia University.

**Emily Murphy Kaur** is director of the Massachusetts Education Partnership (MEP) at the Rennie Center for Education Research & Policy. Emily has dedicated her career to integrating educator and community voice into district-level policy making, ensuring that reforms enacted reflect both local need and classroom realities. In her current position as the MEP director, Emily is responsible for overseeing all aspects of the MEP, a multiyear partnership that has worked with over 120 districts in the Commonwealth to strengthen labor-management relations and school-site operations. Prior to joining the Rennie Center she was a special education teacher with expertise in modifying services, curriculums, and lessons to students with significant disabilities. Through collaborating with diverse partners to ensure that students received the supports necessary to succeed academically and socially, she recognized that the hallmark to successful schooling is in establishing a culture that values and learns from differing perspectives. With this consistently in mind, Emily has worked to establish tools and resources for educators on a variety of topics related to effective team-ing, interest-based bargaining, and strategies for implementing reform together. Emily holds an MA in education policy and social analysis from Teachers College, Columbia University, and an MS in special education from Simmons College.

# Index